The Naturally Sweet Baker

THE
Naturally Sweet
BAKER

150 Decadent Desserts Made with Honey, Maple Syrup, and Other Delicious Alternatives to Refined Sugar

CARRIE DAVIS

WILEY

Published by John Wiley & Sons, Hoboken, NJ

No part of this publication may be reproduced, stored in a retrieval system, or transmitted in any form or by any means, electronic, mechanical, photocopying, recording, scanning, or otherwise, except as permitted under section 107 or 108 of the 1976 United States Copyright Act, without either the prior written permission of the Publisher, or authorization through payment of the appropriate per-copy fee to the Copyright Clearance Center, Inc., 222 Rosewood Drive, Danvers, MA 01923, 978-750-8400, fax 978-750-4470, or on the web at www.copyright.com. Requests to the Publisher for permission should be addressed to the Permissions Department, John Wiley & Sons, Inc., 111 River Street, Hoboken, NJ 07030, 201-748-6011, fax 201-748-6008, email: permcoordinator@wiley.com.

For general information on our other products and services, please contact our Customer Care Department within the United States at 800-762-2974, outside the United States at 317-572-3993 or fax 317-572-4002.

For more information about Wiley products, visit our website at www.wiley.com.

Library of Congress Cataloging-in-Publication Data

Davis, Carrie.
    The naturally sweet baker: 150 decadent desserts made with honey, maple syrup, and other delicious alternatives to refined sugar/ by Carrie Davis.
        p. cm.
    Includes index.
    ISBN 0-02-861257-4 (alk. paper)
    1. Desserts. 2. Baking. 3. Sugar-free diet—Recipes. I. Title.
TX773.D295 1997
641.8'6—dc21   97-17377
                                                      CIP

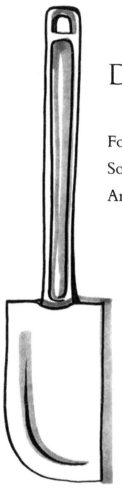

DEDICATION

For my family: Leslie, Mitchell, Sheldon, and our mother, Sonny, whose hearts are even bigger than their appetites! And in loving memory of our father, Robert.

ACKNOWLEDGMENTS

I wish to thank the following people who have helped make this book possible:

David Roth for having such a great idea and for thinking of me to develop it.

Stephanie Ede and Helga Marinzel, whose love and support continually help to guide me through the wonderment of life as I journey to reach my potential.

Evelyn Patterson for her fantastic feasts, generous spirit, and for the use of her ice-cream maker!

Janet Money and Louise Carsh and their friends for being eager recipe testers.

Amy Pataki whose efficiency and attention to detail provided invaluable help with the research and index for this book.

Bonnie Stern for her warm generosity and practical advice.

Pam Koch whose good humor and great nutritional analysis work, even in the midst of her own life's complications, made meeting the deadline a breeze.

Ed Hernstadt, my lawyer, who fine-tuned the contract and always responded quickly and kindly to my ridiculous messages.

Amy Gordon, my editor, whose enthusiasm and candor made the final stages of this project a pleasure.

All the staff at Macmillan, who helped bring this project to fruition.

And to all my friends and colleagues, who selflessly volunteered to taste all my creations.

Table of Contents

Introduction   xi

CHAPTER 1
Understanding Natural Sweeteners
1

CHAPTER 2
Breakfast Sweets
9

CHAPTER 3
Plain and Simple: Crisps, Cobblers,
Compotes, and More
41

CHAPTER 4
Cakes
59

CHAPTER 5

Cookies and Squares
93

CHAPTER 6

Cool and Creamy: Ice Creams,
Sorbets, Mousses, and More
121

CHAPTER 7

Pastry: Pies, Tarts,
Strudels, and More
149

CHAPTER 8

Something Different
181

CHAPTER 9

Foundations and Finishing Touches
209

Source List 235
Index 237

INTRODUCTION

It was June of 1995 and I was in New York City, visiting my brother Mitchell. One evening we had gone to dinner with his friend David Roth, who was working for Macmillan at the time. In between, "Could you pass the hummus?" and "How do you like the pita?" David casually asked if I had any interest in working on a naturally sweetened dessert cookbook. At the time I thought it was an intriguing idea, especially because over the past ten years, preferring not to eat refined sugar, I had adapted some of my standard recipes to be made with natural sweeteners. In addition, during those ten years, I found only a handful of books dedicated to naturally sweetened desserts and even fewer recipes that I would even want to try. I tried to imagine what it would be like to have an entire book filled with decadent desserts that were naturally sweetened.

A few days later, I walked into my brother's office at the James Beard Foundation, only to be greeted with, "David's called a few times wanting to know why I hadn't contacted him. He wants to set up a meeting for you with an editor before you leave." When I finally spoke with him, he explained this was more than just an idea he had been toying with. This was a concept Macmillan was interested in developing and they wanted to move quickly. Needless to say, I spent the next day fine tuning my vision and baking Cream Cheese Cookies (page 103).

What I found most challenging about the idea was that Macmillan wanted a book of dessert recipes that were every bit as delicious as desserts prepared with refined white sugar, but were made with natural sweeteners, such as maple syrup and honey. Most recipes that call for these ingredients are either using them in combination with white sugar or are part of a complete whole foods regimen and are prepared with whole grains and cold-pressed oils—hardly falling into the category of sweet indulgence.

The world of natural sweeteners was not foreign to me. My exposure began in the early eighties, when I read William Duffy's book, *Sugar Blues*. Since that time, my relationship with refined sugar has never been quite the same. Although I may continue to consume it, I do so with the knowledge that there is nothing natural about it. The belief that natural sweeteners are better for you continues to fuel a heated debate between the advocates of whole foods and the conventional nutritionist establishment. Both sides agree, though, that white sugar has been stripped of all of its nutrients. Natural sweeteners, on the other hand, such as honey and maple syrup, are very close to their original forms, enabling them to retain some nutritional value. What always comes into question is whether this is enough to provide any lasting health benefit. Of course, as with most nutritional information, you will have to decide this for yourself.

For me, the real dilemma has always been why there is such a recipe gap between health food and *haute cuisine*. I love desserts, but even when I want to indulge, I do not necessarily want to eat refined sugar. And just because I'm choosing not to eat refined sugar doesn't mean I have suddenly forgotten what good food tastes like.

Keeping this in mind, I went directly to my usual sources for fine baking for inspiration. I thought since natural sweeteners have been around for longer than white sugar as we know it has, it seemed only logical that some experimenting with classic recipes and techniques, which have also been around for centuries, could be adapted to work with these natural ingredients. My hunch was correct and with each successful recipe, I wondered if it had been prepared this way originally.

If you are an experienced baker, some of the techniques will be familiar to you. If you are a novice, you will learn to use both classic and new techniques. In either case, I hope you will not be intimidated. Although I have baked professionally in restaurants and as a caterer, I am self-taught. I owe most of my technical training to Julia Child's television shows and books and to my mother, who learned from her aunt and grandmother. Although my mother didn't bake elaborate desserts, she always started with great recipes. How do you tell a recipe is great before you taste it? Ask anyone in my family and the answer will be the same—butter. What else to look for? Sour cream, perhaps!

I admit, when I first began I was a little concerned about being able to develop as many recipes as had been requested, which was 150. But now that I have so many, my only concern is which ones to leave out. Through some trial and error, I have been able to develop a variety of great-tasting desserts that are sure to rival any sugar-filled recipe.

In many cases, the recipes required significantly smaller amounts of natural sugar than the amount of granulated sugar that was called for originally. But I did not find any standard rule; therefore, you will not find any charts for across-the-board substitutions, as is often the case with other naturally sweetened dessert cookbooks. The sweeteners for each dessert were chosen to produce the best-tasting results. When substitutions can easily be made, they are included in the recipe.

You will also find in many recipes the term "sweeten to taste." My sister was once at the home of a friend who was preparing a packaged-soup mix. She asked her friend if the soup was done. The friend proceeded to get the empty package to check the instructions instead of tasting the soup to determine its doneness. Whether you are cooking or baking, you will sometimes need to taste your ingredients, especially when you are using fruit. Is it sweet or tart? We all know what it is like to sink our teeth into the most beautiful piece of fruit, only to discover it is tasteless. In addition, when you are using a book that is providing an alternative to regular sweeteners, I think there should be room for personal taste. I prefer to let the flavors of the fruit shine through. But if you prefer more sweetness, please do not hesitate to suit your taste.

Ironically, being self-taught may have provided me with the freedom to break the rules that formally trained bakers have held sacred. Even when I would seek the advice of my local maple syrup farmer about the possibilities of using maple syrup in a particular way, he responded with skepticism because he had his own set of rules he followed to produce his different products. So at times I had to throw caution to the wind. My greatest hope for this cookbook is that it will inspire you to do the same—to use my recipes as a beginning from which you will see and taste the possibilities and, in turn, interpret and adjust them to make them your own.

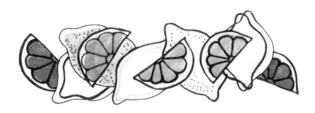

Chapter One

UNDERSTANDING
NATURAL SWEETENERS

WHY NATURAL SWEETENERS?

Natural sweeteners can provide a rich and unique taste to desserts. This is not always the case with standard refined sugars, because they simply provide sweetness without flavor. Natural sweeteners such as maple syrup and honey are closer to their natural form. Natural sugars, therefore, require less energy to be produced than refined sugar. As I see it, using natural sugars may help to sustain the health of our environment.

Refined sugar is produced by boiling down the juice of sugar cane or sugar beets until crystallization takes place. The process strips sugar of its nutrients, leaving behind only "empty calories." Granulated sugar has been linked to diabetes, obesity, and tooth decay, but the average American still consumes more than a pound of sugar every three days.

Many people are under the impression that brown sugar is not white sugar; however, it is white sugar with the addition of molasses, the amount reflected in the color of the brown sugar.

Demerara and turbinado sugars are the crystals from the first stage of sugar refining, and therefore are unrefined natural sweeteners.

Natural sweeteners, on the other hand, contain minerals and vitamins otherwise lost in the refining process. Natural sweeteners are found the world over—Hawaiians use raw pineapple sugar, and East Indians use jaggery, or palm sugar. For the times when you want to indulge your sweet tooth without sacrificing your health—use natural sweeteners.

Maple Syrup

North American aboriginals used maple syrup as a sweetener for centuries before the arrival of the colonists. Today's production of maple syrup is centered in Quebec, Canada, and in the northeastern United States.

In the early spring, when days are warm and nights are cold, maple sap is collected from the sugar maple (*acer saccharum*), the red maple (*acer rubrum*), and the black maple (*acer nigrum*). The sap, which contains only 2 to 3 percent sugar, is boiled down to produce maple syrup. It takes an average of 40 gallons of sap to produce one gallon of syrup—20 gallons when the sap first begins to run and up to 50 gallons at the end of its cycle—and the trees must be at least 30 years old.

The syrup is graded from AA to C (D in Canada). The darker, stronger-flavored grades B and C, are usually recommended for baking. I recommend using extra light to have the sweetness of the syrup without a strong maple flavor. Maple syrup is twice as sweet as granulated sugar. Its boiling point is 212°F and it may be boiled to softball and hardball stages as in candy making, making it ideal for buttercreams and caramel desserts. As for health, maple syrup is a good source of calcium, potassium, and thiamin.

Refrigerate all syrup, even if unopened. Syrup stored in a glass container will keep indefinitely, while that in a tin container keeps for 11 to 12 months. Syrup stored in plastic keeps for 3 to 6 months. It may also be stored indefinitely in the freezer, without freezing. If the syrup is moldy or has begun to ferment, you can rescue it by boiling and skimming the syrup and storing it in a sterilized container.

Maple Sugar

Maple sugar is simply maple syrup boiled down until crystallization takes place. The process first yields maple honey, which is thicker than syrup, and then maple cream or maple butter, which is rich and spreadable. Maple sugar comes either in brick form or as granules, and is most often used in candy making. According to the American Diabetes Association, used in moderation, maple sugar is a simple sugar that does not spike blood glucose.

Maple sugar can be substituted in most recipes calling for granular white sugar or brown sugar. It creams beautifully with butter to produce cakes and cookies with the same texture as classic recipes. It works so well I had to refrain from using it for almost every recipe! Maple butter has been selected for the recipes when the flavor of maple is desired without creating additional liquid.

Since you will definitely want to have plenty of maple sugar on hand, it is easier and more economical to purchase it in bulk through mail order (see Source List, page 235).

Honey

The ancients were mystified by honey: Pliny the Elder thought honey was "saliva emanating from the stars," while Aristotle believed honey could be found only at the end of the rainbow. Today, we know better. According to the National Honey Board, honey is "the nectar and sweet deposits from plants as gathered, modified, and stored in the honeycomb of honey bees."

Common North American honey bees are the Carniolan, Italian, Caucasian, and Buckfast species. Bees collect nectar in their honey sacs, where enzymes kill microbes and the transformation into honey begins. It takes 37,000 honey bee trips to produce one pound of honey.

The chemical and mineral composition of honey varies from type to type and drop to drop, but honey is approximately 30 percent glucose and 40 percent fructose, with the rest being water, proteins, and trace amounts of potassium, calcium, and phosphorous. Many people prefer raw honey since clarified honey, which has been heated to prevent crystallization, has also been stripped of vitamins. In addition to the more popular clover and alfalfa honeys, flavors can include orange blossom, basswood, raspberry, buckwheat, lavender, tupelo, avocado, eucalyptus, wild thyme, prickly pear, chestnut, sage, and sunflower.

During baking, honey has a tendency to sink. It is therefore important to make sure it is thoroughly blended. When using significant amounts of honey in cake recipes, you may need to use what I describe as a "new creaming technique" (see box, page 100). In addition, when adapting white sugar recipes or substituting maple syrup for the sugar, start by reducing the amount of sweetener by at least one half. Honey has 64 calories per 15 ounces, to maple syrup's 40 calories.

Barley Malt Syrup

Barley malt has long been used in making beer and whiskey, but its benefits as a sweetener are now becoming more widely known. Barley malt syrup is high in potassium, is one-third as sweet as granulated sugar, and imparts a dark color to baked goods.

To make barley malt syrup, raw, unhulled barley is first soaked in cold water for two or three days. The barley is forced to sprout and then is kiln dried at 120°F to 180°F. This converts the stored starches into maltose. The malted barley is ground, dipped briefly in an acid solution, and heated with water to make barley malt syrup.

When using it to replace sugar in a recipe, reduce all liquid by one-quarter cup for each cup of barley malt syrup used. Barley malt syrup can be substituted for molasses or honey without adjustment.

Brown Rice Syrup

A sweetening staple in the Orient, where it is known as "*yinnie*," brown rice syrup is a blend of simple and complex carbohydrates. Like barley malt and other grain syrups, brown rice syrup is made sweet by converting starches into maltose. To make brown rice syrup, the rice is ground to meal and cooked with water before enzymes (like those contained in Aspergullus Oryzae mold) are added to break starches down to sugars. The sweet liquid is then boiled down to syrup. Brown rice syrup contains potassium, some protein, and no cholesterol.

In baking, it is best to warm the syrup first, either by itself or by adding it to another warm ingredient like melted butter. When substituting this syrup for other types of liquid sweeteners called for in batter-based recipes, careful adjustments to the dry ingredients are required. In general, more flour and some baking soda are required, otherwise the batter will be too moist. Store the open jars in a cool, dry place. Brown rice syrup is available in many health food stores, especially those that carry products for a macrobiotic diet.

Date Sugar

High in potassium and magnesium and bursting with natural sugars, dates are said to have come from earth that was left over from the creation of Adam. California's Coachella Valley forms the backbone of the North American date industry, producing more than 40 million pounds of dates a year, mainly of the Deglet Noor variety.

Date sugar is commonly made from the Zahidi variety, a firm date originally from Iraq and distinguished by its large seed. The Zahidi has a high invert sugar level, and lends itself well to processing and softening by steam hydration. Date sugar is not entirely dissolvable and can burn quickly. It is best used in fruit fillings. It keeps well in the refrigerator and can be frozen. Date Sugar is available in health-food stores or through mail order.

Molasses

"Slower than molasses in January" wasn't the case in January 1919 when Boston's North End was devastated by the Great Molasses Flood. A holding tank collapsed and 2 million gallons of molasses spewed onto the streets at 35 mph, killing 24 people and injuring 60.

Fortunately, none of the recipes will require you to keep a tank of molasses on hand. Molasses is the liquid remaining after sugar crystals are formed in the refining process. The first boiling yields light molasses, used as a pancake or waffle syrup and equivalent to Britain's golden syrup. The second boiling yields dark molasses (treacle), which is darker, thicker, and less sweet, and used mainly in gingerbread and Boston baked beans. The third boiling yields the somewhat bitter blackstrap molasses, which is widely used in cattle feed and is rich in iron, calcium, and phosphorous.

A sulfur compound is sometimes added to molasses to sterilize and stabilize it. I always recommend using unsulfured molasses in the recipes.

Sucanat

Sucanat is a patented natural sweetener that is high in potassium, iron, and calcium. It is essentially dehydrated molasses. Cane sugar (beet sugar is less savory) is evaporated, the molasses is spun in a centrifuge, and then is dried briefly at 145°F to allow granules to form.

It can be substituted without adjustment for granulated sugar providing you realize it has a much more intense flavor, sometimes leaning towards bitter. I recommend putting it in a food processor fitted with a steel blade for a few minutes to help reduce the size of the granules.

It has a boiling point of 108°F. Sucanat also comes in liquid and honey-like form; however, only the granular form is used throughout this book.

FruitSource

Another patented natural sweetener, FruitSource, uses vacuum pressure to bind grape juice concentrate to whole grain syrup. Because no heat is used, this product retains its full nutritional values, including potassium, iron, and Vitamins A, C, and D. It is metabolized by the body as a complex carbohydrate after two hours, and won't spike blood sugar. As such, it can be used by all types of diabetics. FruitSource caramelizes at 400°F and has a freezing point of 30°F. It can be substituted for granulated sugar in some baked goods. It comes in liquid or granules.

I have used the granular form for recipes when I wanted a dry caramelization effect. I have found, though, that the granules do not cream well with butter; therefore, I have selected it only for recipes not requiring that technique. Although the manufacturer recommends the liquid for baking because it is relatively sweeter and cheaper, I have primarily used this form for recipes in which the fruit juices require more sweetening without wanting to add another identifiable flavor, such as honey or Sucanat. If you develop batter recipes using the liquid form, the fat must be reduced by half, otherwise the batter will be too moist. Both forms can be stored at room temperature, away from direct sunlight, for one year.

Chapter Two

BREAKFAST SWEETS

$\mathcal{A}$lthough one of my favorite breakfast foods is a piece of pie, I have kept that recipe for the pastry section. This chapter is a collection of everyday breakfast sweets like muffins and granola, as well as treats for special occasions (when you have the time for more complicated recipes), like Pecan Sticky Buns or Banana Bread Pudding.

Everyone likes to wake up to the aroma of freshly made baked goods, but few of us want to be up at the crack of dawn working in the kitchen. This chapter contains suggestions for pre-planning ideas, like preparing the batter the night before. By following these suggestions, you can wake up, preheat the oven, and within minutes, have piping hot muffins on the breakfast table. And remember, just because Blueberry Cheese Blintzes is listed here in the breakfast chapter, that doesn't mean you can't serve them for dinner!

Banana Bread Pudding

Makes 6 servings

Multigrain bread layered with bananas makes for a light, naturally sweet breakfast. Using ramekins reduces the baking time so you won't need an extra-early wake-up call. To prevent the bananas from discoloring, peel and slice them as you need them.

3 large eggs

1 cup light cream

1 teaspoon vanilla extract

Pinch of salt

Ten 1-inch-thick slices stale, light-textured multigrain bread

¼ cup maple butter

2 tablespoons maple syrup

3 firm, medium ripe bananas

2 tablespoons unsalted butter, plus more for buttering ramekins

Preheat the oven to 325°F. Butter six ⅔-cup-size ramekins. Have ready a large enough pan to hold the ramekins and water for a bain-marie (see box, page 24).

In a small bowl, whisk together the eggs, cream, vanilla extract, and salt until smooth.

Remove the crust from the bread and spread both sides of each slice lightly with the maple butter. Tear the bread into ½-inch-long pieces. Put 1 teaspoon of maple syrup into the bottom of each ramekin.

Begin slicing the bananas into ¼-inch-thick circles, putting them on the bottom of each ramekin to make a single layer. Distribute half of the bread over the banana layer. Ladle some of the cream mixture over the bread to moisten. Make another layer of bananas and top with the remaining bread. Carefully ladle more cream into each ramekin, making sure to wet all the bread on top and to fill each ramekin to capacity. As the top layer of bread soaks up the cream, use a spoon to gently even out the surface by breaking up some of the larger pieces and moving them around to fill in any gaps.

Spoon 1 teaspoon of melted butter over each pudding. Set the puddings into the pan and fill with enough hot water to reach halfway up the sides of the ramekins. Bake for 30 minutes or until the centers have risen. Serve warm.

Banana Raisin Bran Muffins

Makes 12 jumbo muffins

There is nothing quite like waking up to the perfume of freshly baked muffins, especially when the fragrance of the day is banana! The batter for these golden muffins can be mixed together the night before. Preset the oven timer to turn on in the morning and all you have to do is fill the muffin cups.

1¾ cups buttermilk

1 cup vegetable oil

½ cup unsulfured molasses

½ cup maple syrup

3 large eggs

1 teaspoon vanilla extract

2⅔ cups unbleached all-purpose flour

1 cup cake flour

1 tablespoon baking soda

½ teaspoon salt

2 cups organic wheat bran

¾ cup organic Thompson dark raisins

¼ cup toasted unsalted sunflower seeds

1½ cups very ripe mashed banana

Preheat oven to 375°F. Butter a large 12-cup muffin pan or line the pan with paper muffin cups.

In a large bowl, mix together the buttermilk, oil, molasses, maple syrup, eggs, and vanilla extract. Beat with a whisk until well blended.

In a separate bowl, sift together the flours, baking soda, and salt. Add to the liquid mixture. Add the bran, raisins, and sunflower seeds. Using a wooden spoon, stir all the ingredients together. Fold in the mashed banana.

Spoon the batter into the prepared muffin pan. Bake for about 25 minutes or until a cake tester inserted into the center of the muffin comes out clean.

Note: If usi[ng] smaller muff[in] tins, reduce baking time.

Banana Walnut Bread

Makes 1 loaf

It is hard to find anyone who doesn't like banana bread. For this version, the sweet bananas make this a moist, cakey loaf. If you prefer a different nut, do not hesitate to use it, or try substituting another favorite— chocolate chips.

> ½ cup walnut pieces
>
> 1 cup (2 sticks) unsalted butter, at room temperature
>
> 1¼ cups maple sugar
>
> 4 large eggs
>
> 1¼ cups very ripe mashed banana
>
> 1 teaspoon pure vanilla extract
>
> 2½ cups unbleached all-purpose flour
>
> 1½ teaspoons baking powder
>
> ½ teaspoon salt

Preheat the oven to 350°F. Grease one 6 × 5 × 3-inch loaf pan.

Using a chef's knife and cutting board, coarsely chop the walnuts and place in a shallow baking pan. Bake until lightly toasted, about 5 minutes. Let them cool and set aside.

In the large bowl of an electric mixer, cream together the butter and maple sugar at medium-high speed until light and fluffy, about 4 minutes. Add the eggs two at a time, beating well after each addition. Add the mashed banana and vanilla extract and beat just until incorporated.

In a separate bowl, sift together the flour, baking powder, and salt. By hand or with the electric mixer on low speed, beat the dry ingredients into the banana mixture. Add the toasted nuts and mix until incorporated. Spoon the batter into the prepared loaf pan. Bake for 45 to 50 minutes or until a cake tester inserted into the center comes out clean. Let the bread cool in the pan for about 30 minutes before transferring to a wire rack.

Blueberry Cheese Blintzes

Makes 12 blintzes; 4 servings

For a really decadent Sunday brunch, try cheese blintzes. My mother was never one to skimp on butter, and although we have been told you can bake the blintzes, we like to go all the way and fry them. Prepare the crêpes following the instructions on page 216.

Crêpes

    1 batch Crêpes (page 216)
    Unsalted butter for frying

Cheese filling

    1½ pounds lowfat ricotta cheese
    2 large eggs
    1 tablespoon maple syrup
    1 teaspoon pure vanilla extract
    ¼ teaspoon salt
    1 tablespoon orange zest, finely chopped
    ⅔ cup fresh blueberries, rinsed and stemmed

To serve

    1 batch Blueberry Sauce (page 212)
    1 cup sour cream

In a medium bowl, use a fork to combine the ricotta cheese, eggs, syrup, vanilla extract, and salt until smooth. Mix in the orange zest and the blueberries.

To fill each crêpe, put about 2 tablespoons of the filling in a line about 2 inches from the edge of the crêpe. Roll the edge of the crêpe over the filling, tucking in the sides as you go. Finish with the seam side down.

Just before serving, melt some butter in a large frying pan over medium heat. Place the blintzes in the pan seam side down; do not overcrowd the pan. Cook until golden brown, about 5 minutes. Carefully turn the blintzes over and brown the other side, about 5 minutes. The center should be cooked.

Transfer to a serving platter or individual plates, turning so the seam-side is down. To serve, spoon some of the blueberry sauce over the blitnzes, and top with some sour cream. Serve the remaining sauce and sour cream on the side.

Blueberry Corn Muffins

Makes 12 extra-large muffins

Plump, juicy blueberries are always the perfect flavor to combine with sweet, crunchy cornmeal. In this recipe, the brown rice syrup helps to keep the muffins moist.

½ cup (1 stick) unsalted butter, melted
½ teaspoon salt
¼ cup brown rice syrup
2 cups buttermilk
2 large eggs
2 cups organic cornmeal (see Note)
3 cups unbleached all-purpose flour
5 teaspoons baking powder
2 cups fresh blueberries, rinsed and stemmed

Preheat the oven to 350°F. Butter one 12-cup muffin pan or line pan with paper muffin cups.

In a saucepan, melt the butter. Stir the brown rice syrup into the warm melted butter. Add the buttermilk and eggs. Beat the liquid mixture until blended.

Note: Organic cornmeal is available in some health food stores.

Into a large bowl, measure the cornmeal. Sift together the flour, baking powder, and salt and mix into the cornmeal. Combine the liquid mixture with the dry ingredients and mix together by hand just until everything is moist. Fold in the blueberries and fill the muffin cups.

Bake for about 35 minutes or until a cake tester inserted into the center comes out clean. Remove the muffins from the pan and transfer them to a wire rack to cool.

Blueberry Cornmeal Pancakes

Makes twelve 4-inch pancakes; 4 servings

The cornmeal and semolina give texture and body to these morning treats. The batter works best when it's prepared in advance. Whether you serve them with the Blueberry Sauce on page 212 or just with warm maple syrup, they make waking up fun.

½ cup unbleached all-purpose flour

½ cup yellow cornmeal

½ cup semolina flour

1¾ teaspoons baking powder

½ teaspoon salt

1 large egg

1¼ cups buttermilk

1 teaspoon lemon zest, finely chopped

¾ cup fresh blueberries, rinsed and stemmed

Unsalted butter for frying (optional)

In a medium bowl, mix together the flour, cornmeal, semolina flour, baking powder, and salt. In a separate medium bowl, blend the egg, buttermilk, and lemon zest together. Add to the dry ingredients and mix with a fork just until blended. Let rest at least 1 hour or refrigerate overnight. Just before cooking, gently stir in the blueberries.

Heat a nonstick griddle or frying pan over medium-high heat. Add about a heaping teaspoon of butter to cover the surface of the pan, if desired. Spoon enough batter into the pan to make one 4-inch round cake. Without crowding the pan, repeat with enough batter to fill the pan.

Cook until the bottom of the pancake is browned around the edges and in the center, about 5 minutes. Flip the pancake and continue to cook until juice from the berries begins to appear and the pancake center has cooked through, about 2 minutes. Transfer to a plate and keep warm until all the pancakes are prepared. Serve with more butter and maple syrup.

Buttermilk French Toast with Maple Syrup Peaches

Makes 4 servings

A light-textured, honey-sweetened bread will work best with the tangy flavor of the buttermilk. If you have any leftover Panettone (see page 34) or a homemade challah, save it for this breakfast. When a sweet bread is unavailable, substitute whole milk for the buttermilk.

Peaches

½ cup maple syrup

6 large peaches, peeled and sliced

Pinch of ground cinnamon

French toast

2 cups buttermilk

3 large eggs

2 teaspoons pure vanilla extract

Eight ¾-inch-thick slices sweet egg bread, stale

2 to 4 tablespoons clarified butter

In a large frying pan, bring the maple syrup to a boil. Without crowding the pan, add some of the sliced peaches and cook just until they are heated on both sides, about 1 minute. Meanwhile, remove them from the pan to a heat-resistant bowl. Repeat with the remaining peaches. When all of the peaches are cooked, add the cinnamon to the syrup and cook for another minute. Reserve the syrup until ready to serve.

In a bowl wide enough for dipping a piece of the bread, whisk together the buttermilk, eggs, and vanilla extract. Dip one piece of the bread at a time into the buttermilk mixture, allowing it to absorb the liquid without falling apart. Turn the bread to wet the other side.

Meanwhile, in a clean, large frying pan, heat enough clarified butter to coat the bottom of the pan. When the butter is hot, add the pieces of dipped bread. Cook them until the undersides are golden brown. Turn the pieces and cook the other side, adding butter as necessary. Serve immediately—place two pieces of the toast on each plate, garnish each with the peaches, and serve with the warm syrup.

Granola

Makes about 4 cups; 8 servings

Although there are many granola products promoted as healthful, one bite often indicates they have been prepared with large quantities of sugar. Preparing your own granola is simple and lets you control not only the sweetness and the fat content, but the amount of nuts and fruit as well. Use this recipe as a guide. In a pinch you can add your favorite prepared fruit and nut mixes; just remember they should contain plain, not salted, nuts.

½ cup maple syrup

2 tablespoons vegetable oil

1 teaspoon barley malt syrup

3 cups organic rolled oats

½ cup organic Thompson dark raisins

⅓ cup mix of toasted seeds such as sunflower seeds, pumpkin seeds, sesame seeds

½ cup mix of chopped dried fruit such as papaya, pineapple, apples

2 tablespoons date sugar

Preheat the oven to 325°F. Line a baking sheet with parchment paper.

In a small bowl, mix together the maple syrup, vegetable oil, and barley malt. In a large bowl, put in the oats and pour the syrup mixture over them, tossing to coat. Spread the rolled oat mixture over the prepared baking sheet. Bake until golden brown, about 20 minutes. Stir the oats about every 5 minutes to brown evenly. Let cool.

Combine the browned oats with the raisins, seeds, dried fruit, and date sugar. Store in an airtight container.

Cinnamon Pecan Sticky Buns

Makes 9 large buns

If you want to do something really special for someone or for yourself, take the time to start the day with freshly made sticky buns. Although they are truly at their best when they are baked the same day the dough is made, you can start the dough the night before. I like mine with nuts and raisins, but if you do not, just include whatever you prefer.

You may prepare the dough either by hand or with an electric mixer fitted with a dough hook. I recommend using an electric mixer because this is a very soft and sticky dough. I have had great success kneading it by hand, but this means using more flour for making the dough. Another tip: Flouring your hands keeps the dough from sticking to them.

Dough

¼ cup warm water, no hotter than 115°F

1 tablespoon dry yeast

¾ cup milk

¼ cup sour cream

2 tablespoons (¼ stick) unsalted butter, at room temperature

1 tablespoon honey

1 large egg

3 cups unbleached all-purpose flour, plus more for kneading

½ teaspoon salt

1 tablespoon orange zest, finely chopped

Glaze

1 cup maple syrup

½ cup honey

1 tablespoon unsulfured molasses

¼ cup (½ stick) unsalted butter

1 teaspoon pure vanilla extract

1 tablespoon ground cinnamon

⅔ cup chopped pecans

¼ cup organic Thompson dark raisins

To make the dough by hand: Pour the warm water into a large bowl, add the yeast, and let proof (active yeast will foam and smell yeasty) for 5 minutes. If the yeast does not react, it is dead and you need to get new yeast. Add the milk, sour cream, butter, honey, and egg. Beat to combine. Add the flour, salt, and zest, and begin to incorporate.

Turn the dough onto a lightly floured work surface and knead for 5 minutes. Let the dough rest for about 5 minutes. Continue to knead until the dough becomes very smooth, adding small amounts of flour as needed. Place the dough in a deep buttered bowl and cover with plastic wrap.

To make the dough using an electric mixer: Pour the warm water into a bowl of a mixer fitted with a dough hook. Add the yeast and let proof until it begins to foam, about 5 minutes. Add all of the remaining dough ingredients. With the machine on low speed, mix until the ingredients are incorporated. Turn the machine to high speed and knead for 2 minutes. Let the dough rest for about 5 minutes. Turn the machine on high speed and knead for another 6 minutes, turning the machine off occasionally to scrape down the sides and to turn the dough. The dough should become very smooth.

To remove the dough from the hook, turn the machine off. Add about 1 tablespoon of flour to the dough and turn the machine to medium speed. As soon as the dough begins to pull away from the sides of the bowl, turn the machine off and scoop out the dough. Place the dough into a deep buttered bowl. Cover the bowl with plastic wrap.

Place the bowl in a warm, draft-free area and let rise until double in volume, about 1½ hours (see Note).

Toward the final stage of the first rise, prepare the glaze. In a nonreactive saucepan, combine the maple syrup, honey, molasses, and butter. Cook over high heat until the mixture comes to a boil. Let the mixture reduce slightly to become thicker, about 4 minutes. Remove from the heat and stir in the vanilla extract and cinnamon.

Pour half of the glaze into a 9 × 12 × 2-inch baking pan to cover the entire bottom. Sprinkle the nuts evenly over the glaze. Let the remaining glaze cool to a spreadable consistency.

When the dough has doubled in volume, punch it down and turn it onto a lightly floured work surface. Roll out the dough to form a 20 × 14-inch rectangle. If the dough is difficult to roll to the correct shape, let it rest for 1 minute and continue rolling. Repeat until it reaches the desired size.

Spread the surface of the dough with the remaining glaze, leaving a ½-inch-wide border around the entire rectangle. Sprinkle the dough with the raisins. Beginning with the longer side, loosely roll the dough like a jelly roll. Trim the ends to make a clean edge and cut the log into 9 equal pieces. Working quickly, place each piece cut side down into the pan, forming 3 rows of 3 buns each. To ensure the dough will rise evenly, lightly press down the centers of the buns. Cover the pan loosely with plastic wrap and let the dough double in volume in a warm draft-free place, about 35 minutes.

Meanwhile, preheat the oven to 375°F. When the dough has doubled in volume, remove the plastic wrap and bake for 30 to 40 minutes, or until the glaze is bubbling, the centers sound hollow when tapped, and the tops are browned.

Set a cake rack over a piece of parchment paper or a clean baking sheet to catch drips. Remove the buns from the oven and immediately invert the pan onto the cake rack. Let the buns cool slightly before separating. Serve warm with a really big cup of great coffee!

Note: Before letting the dough rise, you may refrigerate overnight. In the morning, bring the dough to room temperature before proceeding.

Jelly Doughnuts

Makes eighteen 3-inch doughnuts

Coffee and doughnuts may not be the most healthful breakfast, but it's nice to live dangerously once in a while. You may prepare the dough either by hand or with an electric mixer fitted with a dough hook. I recommend using an electric mixer because this is a very soft and sticky dough. I have had great success kneading it by hand, but this means using more flour for making the dough. Another tip: Flouring your hands keeps the dough from sticking to them.

Dough

¼ cup warm water, no hotter than 115°F

1 tablespoon dry yeast

1 cup milk

2 tablespoons (¼ stick) unsalted butter, at room temperature

1 tablespoon honey

1 large egg

3 cups unbleached all-purpose flour, plus more for kneading

¾ teaspoon salt

1 quart vegetable oil for deep frying

Filling

1 cup all-fruit spread

½ cup maple sugar for dipping (optional)

To make the dough by hand: Pour the warm water into a large bowl, add the yeast, and let proof (active yeast will foam and smell yeasty) for 10 minutes. If the yeast does not react, it is dead and you need to get new yeast. Add the milk, butter, honey, and egg. Beat to combine. Add the flour and salt and begin to incorporate.

Turn the dough onto a lightly floured work surface and knead for 5 minutes. Let the dough rest for 6 minutes. Continue to knead until the dough becomes very smooth, adding small amounts of flour as needed. Place the dough in a deep buttered bowl and cover with plastic wrap.

To make the dough using an electric mixer: Pour the warm water into the bowl of an electric mixer fitted with a dough hook. Add the yeast and let proof until it begins to foam, about 5 minutes. Add all of the remaining dough ingredients. With the machine on low speed, mix until the ingredients are incorporated. Turn the machine to high speed and knead for 2 minutes. Let the dough rest for about 5 minutes. Turn the machine on high speed and knead for about 6 minutes, turning the machine off occasionally to scrape down the sides and to turn the dough. The dough should become very smooth.

To remove the dough from the hook, turn the machine off. Add about one tablespoon of flour to the dough and turn the machine to medium speed. As soon as the dough begins to pull away from the sides of the bowl, turn the machine off and scoop out the dough. Place the dough into a deep buttered bowl. Cover the bowl with plastic wrap.

Place the bowl in a warm, draft-free area and let rise until doubled in volume, about 1½ hours (see Note).

Transfer the dough to a lightly floured work surface. Using a rolling pin, roll the dough to about 1 inch thick. Using a 2-inch-round biscuit cutter, cut out the doughnuts. Cover loosely with plastic wrap. Let rest for about 15 minutes.

Meanwhile, in a deep fryer or a deep, heavy saucepan, heat the oil to a constant 375°F on a frying thermometer. Or test by dropping about 1 teaspoon of batter into the oil. The oil should immediately sizzle around the batter. (If the oil begins to smoke, it is too hot, and you should reduce the heat slightly.) Gently drop the doughnuts into the oil, keeping in mind they will expand considerably. Do not crowd the pan. When the undersides are browned, about 2 minutes, turn the doughnuts over to cook the other side until brown, about 2 minutes.

Use tongs to remove the doughnuts from the oil and tap them on paper towel to remove any excess oil. Stand the doughnuts upright on a wire rack set over paper towel to catch any dripping oil. Let cool.

Note: Before letting the dough rise, you may refrigerate it overnight. In the morning bring the dough to room temperature before proceeding.

Breakfast Sweets

Meanwhile, transfer the fruit spread to a pastry bag fitted with a small, plain tip. Put the maple sugar into a bowl or onto a small plate. When the doughnuts are cool enough to handle, insert a bamboo skewer through one side of each doughnut, but do not go through to the other side. Insert the tip of the pastry bag into the skewed hole and gently pipe some spread into the doughnut. Dip each doughnut in the maple sugar, coating it on all sides. Work quickly to finish the remaining doughnuts. Serve immediately.

Bain-marie

Bain-marie is the French name for a hot-water bath traditionally used in the preparation of dishes like custards, puddings, and terrines. It is similar to the concept of a double boiler, but the water is never allowed to boil. Most often, the bain-marie is placed in the oven. The steam that rises from the hot-water bath adds moisture to baked items and creates velvety textured foods.

To prepare a bain-marie, place the batter-filled pan or ramekins into a second, larger pan with sides. The larger pan is then filled with warm water to about halfway up the sides of the smaller pan. Follow baking directions as given in the recipe. The water should not be allowed to boil or diminish; control the water temperature and level by adding cool water when necessary.

Lemon Blueberry Muffins

Makes 16 large muffins

Fresh, plump blueberries and tangy lemon are always tastes worth waking up for! In separate bowls, get the dry and liquid ingredients ready the night before. Store in the refrigerator and all you have to do in the morning, aside from getting out of bed, is preheat the oven.

2½ cups unbleached all-purpose flour

2 cups hard whole wheat flour (see box, page 26)

4½ teaspoons baking powder

¾ cup (1½ sticks) unsalted butter

1½ cups milk

1 cup sour cream

3 large eggs

½ cup maple syrup

1 tablespoon lemon zest, finely chopped

1 teaspoon pure vanilla extract

2 cups fresh blueberries, rinsed and stemmed

Preheat the oven to 350°F. Butter a large muffin pan or line with paper muffin cups.

In a large bowl, sift together the flours and baking powder. Stir in the whole wheat flour. Using a pastry cutter or two knives cut in the butter until it resembles coarse meal.

In a separate bowl, beat together the milk, sour cream, eggs, maple syrup, zest, and vanilla extract. Pour the liquid mixture into the dry ingredients and mix with a wooden spoon just until the ingredients are wet; do not overmix. Fold in the blueberries.

Fill the muffin cups three-quarters full and bake in the preheated oven for 30 to 35 minutes or until a cake tester inserted into the center comes out clean. Remove from the pan and cool on a wire rack.

Note: If using a smaller sized muffin pan, reduce the baking time.

The Soft and Hard of It

There are two types of whole wheat flour: soft and hard. Soft whole wheat flour is produced from summer-harvested wheat and has a lower gluten content. It is recommended for pastries and cakes. Hard whole wheat flour is produced from the winter wheat harvest. Its high gluten content makes it desirable for making breads.

Gluten is the protein in wheat. If moistened, such as in a dough, and then kneaded, the gluten develops into thin, flexible, web-like strands. Carbon dioxide is trapped between the strands as they stretch and expand. Well-developed webs of gluten are ideal for bread-making, since they enable the dough to rise and maintain its shape. Conversely, to create flaky pastry or delicate cakes, short strands of gluten are more desirable.

For muffins, I recommend using hard flour because its gluten content helps to produce a muffin with a moister crumb.

Lemon–Sweet Potato Biscuits

Makes 12 biscuits

This is a great way to use any leftover sweet potatoes you may have. Otherwise, you can always bake the sweet potato while you are baking something else for dinner—that way it will be ready to use in the morning. The sweet potato adds great flavor in addition to creating a beautiful orange-colored, tender biscuit.

> **1 large sweet potato, about 10 ounces**
> **2½ cups unbleached all-purpose flour, plus additional for kneading**
> **4 teaspoons baking powder**
> **1 teaspoon salt**
> **¼ cup (½ stick) unsalted butter, chilled**
> **1 tablespoon lemon zest, finely chopped**
> **½ cup buttermilk**
> **1 tablespoon barley malt syrup**

Preheat the oven to 400°F. Butter or line a large cookie sheet with parchment.

Bake the sweet potato until tender, about 35 minutes. Let cool. Remove the skin and purée either in a blender or a food processor. You should have 1 scant cup of purée. Set aside.

In a large bowl, sift together the flour, baking powder, and salt. Cut the butter into the flour until it resembles coarse meal. This may be done either by hand using a pastry cutter or with a food processor. If using the food processor, put the ingredients into the work bowl fitted with the steel blade and pulse the machine on and off about 10 times. Transfer the ingredients to a large bowl. Mix in the lemon zest.

In a separate bowl, mix the sweet potato purée with the buttermilk and the barley malt syrup until thoroughly blended. Add the sweet potato mixture to the dried ingredients. Using a fork, combine the ingredients, allowing the flour to absorb the moisture from the wet ingredients. Use your hands to gently knead the dough 3 to

4 times, just until it holds together. If the dough is very wet, add small amounts of flour, about a teaspoon at a time.

Turn the dough onto a lightly floured work surface. Sprinkle the top of the dough very lightly with flour and roll out to 1 inch thick. Cut into desired shapes and put onto the prepared cookie sheet. Bake for about 13 minutes or until the bottoms are lightly browned and the centers are cooked through. Serve warm or cooled.

Molasses Raisin Bran Muffins

Makes 12 jumbo muffins

Dark as night and sweet as sunshine, these muffins are a great start to any day. The crunchy top leads to a moist center enhanced with bursts of plump raisins. Who would believe these take minutes to prepare? Try making the batter the night before, refrigerate, and bake the muffins fresh in the morning.

- **2 cups buttermilk**
- **1 cup vegetable oil**
- **1 cup unsulphured molasses**
- **3 large eggs**
- **1 teaspoon pure vanilla extract**
- **2⅔ cups unbleached all-purpose flour**
- **1 cup cake or pastry flour**
- **1 tablespoon baking soda**
- **½ teaspoon salt**
- **2 cups organic wheat bran**
- **1½ cups organic Thompson dark raisins**

Preheat oven to 375°F. Butter a large 12-cup muffin pan or line muffin cups with paper liners.

In a large bowl, mix together the buttermilk, oil, molasses, eggs, and vanilla extract. Beat with a whisk until well blended.

Note: If using smaller muffin tins, reduce the baking time.

In another large bowl, sift together the flours, baking soda, and salt. Stir into the liquid mixture. Add the bran and raisins. Using a wooden spoon, stir all the ingredients together.

Spoon the batter into the prepared muffin pan or cups. Bake for about 25 minutes or until a cake tester inserted into the center of the muffin comes out clean.

Oatmeal Nutmeg Pancakes

Makes eight 5-inch pancakes

When most people hear "oatmeal," they think of a bowl of mushy porridge. But here, rolled oats and oatmeal work together to create a light, airy pancake with subtle texture, lots of B vitamins, and fiber. My mother always fried pancakes in butter, creating a flavor I have grown to prefer, but for a lower-fat version, use a nonstick griddle and hold the butter.

1 cup unbleached all-purpose flour
½ cup organic rolled oats
¼ cup organic oatmeal (see Note)
1 teaspoon baking powder
½ teaspoon salt
¼ teaspoon freshly grated nutmeg
2 large egg yolks
1 cup whole milk
½ teaspoon pure vanilla extract
2 large egg whites, at room temperature
2 tablespoons unsalted butter (optional)

In a medium bowl, mix together the flour, rolled oats, oatmeal, baking powder, salt, and nutmeg. In a separate medium bowl, whisk together the egg yolks, milk, and vanilla extract. Add the liquid mixture to the dry ingredients, stirring with a fork just until blended.

In a clean bowl, beat the egg whites until stiff but not dry. Fold the whites into the oatmeal batter.

Heat a nonstick griddle or frying pan over medium–high heat. Test by placing a few drops of water onto the griddle—if the water sizzles, the griddle is the right temperature. Add enough butter to lightly coat the surface of the pan, if desired. Allowing for a little spreading, spoon enough batter into the pan to make one 5-inch disc. Repeat until the pan is full, but not crowded. Cook until holes appear on the surface of each pancake and flip to lightly brown the other side, about 1 minute. Transfer to a warm plate. Serve warm with plenty of maple syrup.

Orange Cranberry Muffins

Makes 16 large muffins

For a tart-tasting fruit muffin, freeze fresh cranberries when in season during the fall to use when they are least expected. For best results, defrost the berries before using.

- 4½ cups unbleached all-purpose flour
- 4½ teaspoons baking powder
- ¾ cup (1½ sticks) unsalted butter
- 1½ cups milk
- 1 cup sour cream
- 3 large eggs
- ½ cup maple syrup
- 1 tablespoon orange zest, finely chopped
- 1 teaspoon pure vanilla extract
- 2 cups cranberries

Preheat the oven to 350°F. Butter a large muffin pan or line with paper muffin cups.

In a large bowl, sift together the flour and baking powder. Using a pastry cutter or two knives, cut in the butter until it resembles coarse meal. In a separate large bowl, beat together the milk, sour cream, eggs, maple syrup, orange zest, and vanilla extract. Pour the liquid mixture into the dry ingredients and mix with a wooden spoon just until the ingredients are wet; do not overmix. Fold in the cranberries.

Fill the muffin cups three-quarters full and bake about 25 minutes or until a cake tester inserted into the center comes out clean. Remove from the pan and cool on a wire rack.

Note: If using smaller sized muffin pan, reduce the baking time.

Oatmeal Pear Muffins

Makes 12 jumbo muffins

This combination of sweet pears and currants makes these treats a welcome surprise first thing in the morning! Choose ripe, but firm, pears. If the perfect pears are not available, a firm apple, such as a Golden Delicious or a Northern Spy, will be just as welcome.

> 2 cups buttermilk, at room temperature
> 1 cup (2 sticks) unsalted butter, melted
> ¾ cup maple syrup
> ¼ cup barley malt syrup
> 3 large eggs
> ½ teaspoon pure vanilla extract
> 2⅔ cups unbleached all-purpose flour
> 1 cup organic whole wheat flour
> 1 tablespoon baking soda
> 2 teaspoons ground cinnamon
> ¼ teaspoon ground cardamom
> ¼ teaspoon ground nutmeg
> ½ teaspoon salt
> 2 cups organic rolled oats
> 1 tablespoon orange zest, finely chopped
> 2 ripe pears, peeled and diced
> 1 cup dried currants

Preheat the oven to 375°F. Butter a large muffin pan or line the pan with paper muffin cups.

In a large bowl, mix together the buttermilk, butter, maple syrup, barley malt syrup, eggs, and vanilla extract until well blended.

In a separate large bowl, sift together the flours, baking soda, spices, and salt. Mix in the rolled oats and orange zest. Add the dry ingredients to the liquid mixture. Using a wooden spoon, stir all the ingredients together just until blended. Fold in the diced pears and the currants.

Spoon the batter into the prepared muffin pan. Bake for 25 to 30 minutes or until a cake tester inserted into the muffins comes out clean.

Note: If usin smaller muff tins, the bak time should reduced.

Orange Currant Scones

Makes 12 scones

Whether it's breakfast or high tea, these light and flaky scones will make you wonder just how one gets to Buckingham Palace. Not to mention, where is the clotted cream?

3 cups unbleached all-purpose flour
2½ teaspoons baking powder
½ teaspoon baking soda
½ teaspoon salt
2 tablespoons maple sugar
¾ cup (1½ sticks) unsalted butter, chilled
2 tablespoons orange zest, finely chopped
⅔ cup dried currants
1 cup buttermilk

Preheat the oven to 425°F. Butter a large cookie sheet or line it with parchment paper.

In the bowl of a food processor fitted with the steel blade, combine the flour, baking powder, baking soda, salt, and maple sugar. To blend the ingredients, pulse the food processor 3 to 5 times for a few seconds each time.

Cut the butter into 1-inch cubes. Uncover the bowl of the processor and place the butter on top of the dry ingredients, distributing it evenly. To cut the butter into the flour mixture, replace the cover, and again by using a pulsing action, turn the machine on and off 8 to 10 times. Continue just until the mixture resembles coarse meal. Do not overprocess. If the butter begins to melt, refrigerate until firm.

Turn the mixture into a large mixing bowl. Add the orange zest and currants and stir to distribute. Pour in the buttermilk. Using a fork, blend the ingredients to absorb the liquid. At this point, the ingredients may look very dry. Press the mixture together with your hands. This will allow you to feel the moisture in the dough. Once you have most of the flour incorporated, knead the dough 2 or 3 times, either in the bowl or on a flat surface.

Roll the dough into a 12 × 16-inch rectangle, 1 inch thick, on a lightly floured surface. Use a knife to cut the dough to make clean straight edges. To shape into triangles, divide the width of the dough into thirds. Cut each third in half horizontally to create 6 squares. Cut each square diagonally.

Place scones 1 inch apart on the prepared cookie sheet. Bake in the middle of the oven for about 13 minutes. Remove to a wire rack and cool slightly. Serve warm.

Handle with Care

The secret to making tender scones and biscuits is to spend as little time as possible working with the dough. Make sure the butter is well chilled. Choose a shape such as triangles that lets you utilize as much of the dough as possible the first time it is rolled out. The less the dough is handled, the better and more tender the scones will be.

Panettone

Makes 2 large loaves

It was late December 1993 when I received a telephone call from my brother in New York. He was excited about just having baked panettone *to give as Christmas gifts to his friends. As he described his triumph of a towering, buttery, fig-and-white chocolate-studded bread, I began to come down with a family condition known as "food envy." Even though I shared in my brother's accomplishment of preparing this traditional Italian holiday bread—which is a two-day event—I was once again reminded of how far away we lived from one another. In addition, I couldn't help being reduced to the two-year-old in me who had to blurt out, "Where's mine?"*

Imagine my surprise when the next morning the door bell rang and it was Federal Express. The delivery man handed me a package with a customs declaration of "home-baked goods." There was no duty, perhaps because there was not enough room to indicate the true value of the package! A new annual sibling tradition had begun.

In 1995, I sent my brother my naturally sweetened version based on Carol Field's traditional method in The Italian Baker. *Traditionally, the recipe calls for candied citron, but I have increased the amount of zest and added dates to create my own fresh flavor.*

Although there are a number of steps to making panettone, *it is its slow rise that makes it necessary to start the preparations a day ahead. For best results, I recommend using a heavy-duty electric mixer. The shape of the pan is also very important; to create a really tall and light bread the pan needs to have tall, straight sides. If a panettone pan is not available, the bread can be made in two 2-pound coffee tins or in buttered brown paper lunch bags.*

Filling

1¼ cups organic Thompson dark raisins

½ cup dried whole dates, chopped

½ cup dark rum

⅓ cup orange zest, finely chopped

⅓ cup lemon zest, finely chopped

Sponge

⅓ cup of warm water

2½ teaspoons active dried yeast

½ cup unbleached all-purpose flour

First dough

3 tablespoons warm water

2½ teaspoons active dry yeast

2 large eggs, at room temperature

2 tablespoons honey

¼ cup (½ stick) unsalted butter, at room temperature

Second dough

2 large eggs

3 large egg yolks

⅔ cup honey

1½ teaspoons pure vanilla extract

1 teaspoon of salt

1 cup (2 sticks) unsalted butter, at room temperature

About 3 cups unbleached all-purpose flour, plus about ¾ cup for
   kneading

To prepare the filling: Put the raisins, dates, and rum in a nonreactive bowl. Cover and let soak until the final stages of the dough preparation, at which time add the orange and lemon zest to the macerated fruits.

   To prepare the sponge: Pour the warm water into a small bowl, add the yeast, and let proof (active yeast will foam and smell yeasty) for 10 minutes. If the yeast does not react, it is dead and you need to get new yeast. Stir in the flour. Cover the bowl with plastic wrap and let rise until double in volume, 20 to 30 minutes.

To prepare the first dough: In the bowl of an electric mixer, stir the water and yeast together and let proof until creamy, about 10 minutes. Add the sponge, eggs, and honey and beat to combine using the paddle attachment. Add the butter and beat until the dough is smooth, about 3 minutes. Cover the bowl with plastic wrap and let rise until double in volume, about 1¼ hours.

To prepare the second dough: Add the eggs, egg yolks, honey, vanilla extract, and salt to the first dough and mix using the paddle attachment until well combined. Add the butter and mix until the dough is smooth. Add the flour and continue mixing until the dough resembles cookie dough. Using the dough hook, knead the dough until it becomes smoother and soft, about 2 minutes. Transfer the dough to a lightly floured work surface and knead by hand to finish, adding flour as necessary.

Place the dough in a very large, lightly oiled bowl and cover with plastic wrap. Let the dough rise until it has tripled in volume, about 2½ to 4 hours.

On a lightly floured work surface, divide the dough in half. Flatten each piece into an oval shape. Spread each oval with one-fourth of the filling. Roll the dough like a jelly roll. Flatten the log to create as much surface as possible and spread another one-fourth of the filling over each dough. Roll up the dough again.

Butter 2 panettone pans or two 2-pound coffee cans. Cut parchment paper circles to fit the bottom of the baking pans. Butter the circles and press them into the inside of the pans. If using paper bags, select 2 large, square-bottom brown paper lunch bags. To create more stability, fold back the top edge, about 3 inches down. Brush the insides of the bags with melted butter. Place the filled bags on a cookie sheet to bake.

Shape each dough into a ball and place into the prepared baking mold. Cut an X at the top of each loaf. Cover the dough with a damp cloth and let rise until double in volume, about 2 hours.

While the dough is rising, preheat the oven to 400°F. Just before baking, cut the X again. Bake for 10 minutes. Reduce the temperature to 375°F and bake for another 10 minutes. Reduce the temperature to 350°F and bake until a tester inserted into the center comes out clean, about 25 minutes. Let cool in the mold on a wire rack for 30 minutes. To prevent the breads from collapsing, remove them from the mold and cool on their sides. If using the paper bags, just let them cool in the bag on their sides.

Sour Cream Marble Pound Cake

Makes 1 cake; 12 servings

This is a rich, moist cake marbled with dark chocolate and maple and finished with a tangy glaze. It's perfect for a mid-morning or an afternoon coffee break.

Cake

 1 cup grain-sweetened chocolate (see Note)
 1 cup (2 sticks) unsalted butter, at room temperature
 2 cups maple sugar
 6 large eggs
 3 cups unbleached all-purpose flour
 ¼ teaspoon salt
 ¼ teaspoon baking soda
 1 cup sour cream
 2 teaspoons pure vanilla extract
 2 tablespoons fresh orange juice
 1 tablespoon orange zest, finely chopped

Glaze

 1 tablespoon rum
 ¼ cup fresh orange juice
 1 tablespoon honey
 1 tablespoon brown rice syrup

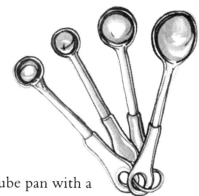

Preheat the oven to 325°F. Butter one 10-inch tube pan with a removable bottom.

Melt the chocolate in a small bowl set over simmering water. Set aside.

In the large bowl of an electric mixer, cream the butter and maple sugar until the mixture is thick and pale, at least 6 minutes. Beat in the eggs one at a time, making sure to beat for a full minute after each addition.

In a large bowl, sift together the flour, salt, and baking soda. With the machine running at low speed, add the dry ingredients to the butter mixture, alternating with the sour cream. Scrape down the sides as needed to make sure nothing remains unbeaten. Add the vanilla extract, orange juice, and zest. Pour half the batter into the pan.

Add the melted chocolate to the remaining batter and stir until blended. To create the marble effect, spoon the chocolate batter onto the orange batter, and with each spoonful, cut down and swirl the chocolate through.

Bake the cake for 1 hour or until a tester inserted into the cake comes out clean. Remove from the oven and leave in the pan to glaze. Glaze while the cake is warm.

To prepare the glaze, combine the rum, juice, honey, and rice syrup in a small saucepan. Bring the mixture to a boil. Pierce the cake multiple times with a cake tester. Brush the glaze over all of the cake letting it run down the sides. To remove the cake from the pan, run a knife around the sides of the pan and lift the bottom. Cut into 12 slices. (This cake is best served the day after it is made.)

Note: You can use either grain-sweetened chocolate chips or baker's squares available from Sunspire. See Source List (page 235).

Spiced Mango Bread

Makes 1 loaf

Sweet, ripe mangos make this a super-moist bread, while the spices complete the exotic tropical flavor.

1 cup (2 sticks) unsalted butter, at room temperature

1 cup maple sugar

4 large eggs

1 ripe large mango

2½ cups unbleached all-purpose flour

1½ teaspoons baking powder

½ teaspoon ground cinnamon

½ teaspoon ground cardamom

¼ teaspoon freshly ground nutmeg

¼ teaspoon ground cloves

½ teaspoon salt

Preheat the oven to 350°F. Butter one 9 × 5 × 3-inch loaf pan.

In a large bowl of an electric mixer, cream together the butter and maple sugar at medium-high speed until light and fluffy, about 4 minutes. Add the eggs 2 at a time, beating well after each addition.

Peel the mango and separate the flesh from the pit without removing the stringy fibers. In a blender or food processor, coarsely chop the mango to produce about 1 scant cup of both purée and chunks. Beat the mango into the creamed mixture.

In a separate large bowl, sift together the flour, baking powder, all of the spices, and salt. Either by hand or with the electric mixer on low speed, beat the dry ingredients into the mango mixture. Spoon the batter into the prepared loaf pan.

Bake for 55 to 60 minutes. A cake tester inserted into the center may come out clean after about 45 minutes, but to prevent the cake from falling, make sure the top of the cake no longer looks wet before removing it from the oven. Let the bread cool in the pan for about 30 minutes before transferring to a wire rack.

Chapter Three

PLAIN AND SIMPLE: CRISPS, COBBLERS, COMPOTES, AND MORE

*𝒜*s the title suggests, this chapter is dedicated to unpretentious, fruit-based desserts, such as crisps, cobblers, and compotes. Let the fruit be your guide. Select the season's best and sweeten the recipes to your taste. Serve these treats warm or cold in winter, spring, summer, or fall.

Apple Crisp

Makes 6 servings

If you're looking for a simple dessert that only takes a few moments to make, here it is. Apples are a classic, but you can mix up all different combinations of fresh and dried fruits.

Fruit filling

- 6 large baking apples (see box, page 153)
- 1 tablespoon cornstarch
- 1 teaspoon cinnamon
- ½ cup unsweetened apple juice
- 1 tablespoon unsalted butter

Topping

- 1 cup rolled oats
- 1 cup unbleached all–purpose flour
- ½ teaspoon baking soda
- Pinch of salt
- ½ cup (1 stick) unsalted butter
- ¼ cup brown rice syrup
- 1 teaspoon pure vanilla extract

Preheat the oven to 350°F. Butter a shallow 1-quart baking dish.

Peel, core, and slice the apples into ¼-inch-thick wedges and put in a large bowl. Toss the apples with the cornstarch and cinnamon. Put the apples into the prepared baking dish. Pour in the apple juice and dot the apples with 1 tablespoon butter.

In a medium bowl, mix together the rolled oats, flour, baking soda, and salt.

In a small saucepan, melt the butter over medium heat. Remove from the heat. Stir the brown rice syrup and vanilla extract into the melted butter. Pour the liquid mixture into the dry ingredients and stir until thoroughly blended. Spoon the batter evenly over the top of the apples.

Bake for about 50 minutes. The juices from the apples should be bubbling. If the top begins to brown before the apples are done, remove the dish from the oven and cover it with aluminum foil. Pierce the foil with a fork to let the steam escape. Return the crisp to the oven and continue baking until the apples are fully cooked without loosing their shape. Serve warm or chilled.

Apple Rhubarb Crisp

Makes 8 servings

The tart flavor of the rhubarb is balanced by the sweetness of the Sucanat.

6 large apples, peeled and cored (see box, page 153)
1 cup Sucanat
4 stalks rhubarb, cut into ½-inch-long pieces
2 tablespoons tapioca flour or cornstarch
½ teaspoon ground cinnamon
⅛ teaspoon ground cloves
⅛ teaspoon ground allspice
Pinch of freshly grated nutmeg
½ cup (1 stick) unsalted butter, chilled
¾ cup unbleached all-purpose flour
¾ cup organic rolled oats
Pinch of salt

Preheat the oven to 350°F. Butter a 2-quart baking dish.

Slice the apples into ½-inch-thick wedges and place them in a large bowl. Add ½ cup of the Sucanat, reserving the remaining sweetener for the topping. Add the rhubarb, tapioca flour, cinnamon, cloves, allspice, and nutmeg and toss to combine. Transfer the fruit to the baking dish.

Cut the butter into the flour until it resembles coarse meal. This may be done either with a food processor or by hand using a pastry cutter. If using the food processor, put the ingredients into the bowl fitted with the steel blade. Pulse the machine on and off about 10 times.

Add the the rolled oats and salt; toss to combine. Spoon the flour mixture over the fruit and bake for 50 to 60 minutes, or until the juices from the fruit are bubbling around the edges and in the center of the dish. Watch carefully to be sure the Sucanat doesn't burn. If the top is getting too brown, cover it with a piece of aluminum foil. Pierce the aluminum foil a few times with a fork to allow the steam to escape. Serve warm.

The Naturally Sweet Baker

Applesauce

Makes 6 servings

My sister Leslie and I have a serious ongoing debate. She prefers her applesauce made with Macintosh apples; I prefer Northern Spy. Although there seems little chance of resolution, the debate process is quite flavorful. In her home, she makes it the way she likes it, and vice versa. Needless to say, we still manage to eat plenty of applesauce, regardless of the variety of apple or in whose house it's made!

A little liquid is needed to get started. What looks like it will produce a ton of applesauce reduces down to very little as it cooks. Applesauce can be frozen in an airtight container for up to 2 months.

10 medium apples, peeled, cored, and coarsely chopped

¼ cup apple juice, not from concentrate, or water

½ teaspoon ground cinnamon (optional)

½ teaspoon pure vanilla extract (optional)

In a heavy saucepan, combine the apples and apple juice. Bring the mixture to a soft boil over medium heat. Reduce the heat to medium-low. Stirring occasionally, continue cooking until the apples fall apart and create a sauce. Add the cinnamon and vanilla extract, if desired.

The consistency will reflect the variety of apples used: Macintosh will produce a smoother sauce, while Northern Spy will be lumpy. For a very smooth sauce, pass the mixture through a ricer or purée in a food processor. Serve warm or chilled.

Baked Apples

Makes 6 servings

I'm not sure which is more "plain and simple," baked apples or applesauce, but both are equally delicious.

6 medium baking apples (see box, page 153)
½ cup organic Thompson dark raisins
¼ cup date sugar
1 teaspoon cinnamon
2 tablespoons unsalted butter, melted (optional)
½ cup apple juice, not from concentrate, or water

Preheat the oven to 350°F. Have ready a baking dish large enough to hold the apples closely together.

Slice off the tops of the apples. Using an apple corer, core the apples, making sure to keep the apples in one piece. Put the apples cut side up in the baking dish. In a medium bowl, mix together the raisins, date sugar, cinnamon, and melted butter, if desired. Spoon the raisin mixture into the center of each apple. Pour the apple juice into the bottom of the pan.

Bake for about 30 minutes or until the apples are soft. Watch carefully to prevent the apples from bursting (see Note). Remove from the oven and let cool. These may be served warm or chilled. I prefer them reheated, the day after they have been baked.

Note: In the event the apples do burst and you were serving them to company, no one has to know. Scrape the flesh from the skins and serve as applesauce!

te: The brown
rice syrup
makes a very
moist batter,
and the
topping may
brown before
the batter is
thoroughly
ooked. When
e fruit juices
in the center
ble, the batter
has reached
the proper
mperature. If
the topping
wns before the
enter bubbles,
cover with
uminum foil
hat is pierced
let the steam
escape, and
continue
baking.

Blueberry-Nectarine Cornbread Cobbler

Makes 10 servings

Nectarines are often overlooked in the search for peaches when it comes to desserts. They may owe their pink flesh to their hybridization with peaches, but unlike peaches, they have a smooth skin and firm texture. This makes them especially easy to bake with because there is no need to peel them before adding them to recipes.

As with the Blueberry Corn Muffin recipe on page 15, the brown rice syrup will help to keep the interior of the cobbler moist, but you will want to bake it long enough to create a crispy top.

Fruit filling

2 pints fresh blueberries, rinsed and stemmed

6 nectarines, sliced into ½-inch-thick wedges

⅓ cup Sucanat

1 teaspoon ground cinnamon

2 tablespoons cornstarch

1 tablespoon lemon zest, finely chopped

Cornbread topping

1 cup cornmeal

1 cup unbleached all-purpose flour

½ teaspoon ground cinnamon

2½ teaspoons baking powder

¼ teaspoon salt

6 tablespoons (¾ stick) unsalted butter

2 tablespoons brown rice syrup

1 tablespoon barley malt syrup

½ cup buttermilk

1 large egg

Preheat the oven to 375°F. Butter one 8 × 12-inch baking pan.

In a large bowl, combine the blueberries, sliced nectarines, Sucanat, cinnamon, cornstarch, and lemon zest and pour into the prepared baking dish.

To prepare the cornmeal topping, mix together the cornmeal, flour, cinnamon, baking powder, and salt in a clean large bowl. In a small saucepan, melt the butter. Remove from the heat. Add the rice and barley malt syrups to the warm butter and stir until blended. Stir the buttermilk into the syrup mixture and beat in the egg. Mix the liquid mixture into the dry ingredients and stir with a fork until the batter is blended; do not overmix.

Drop the batter by spoonfuls on top of the fruit. Bake for about 50 minutes or until the fruit is bubbling along the sides and in the center.

Cherry Kumquat Compote

Makes about 3 cups; 6 servings

My first kumquat was a garnish for a petit four *at Le Cirque, a posh midtown-Manhattan restaurant. In addition to the kumquat's fun name, it is a cute little citrus fruit with much flavor. The tartness is easily balanced with sweet cherries and fragrant honey. If orange blossom honey is available, this is a perfect time to use it.*

1⅓ cups water
¾ cup honey, preferably orange blossom
¾ pound stemmed kumquats
1 cup pitted cherries
2 tablespoons orange or cherry liqueur (kirsch)

In a medium nonreactive saucepan, combine the water and the honey and bring to a boil, cooking over high heat. Meanwhile, slice the kumquats in half crosswise. Remove the seeds and combine with the cherries. Add the fruit to the boiling water and reduce the heat to medium-low. Cook the fruit for 5 minutes.

Using a slotted spoon, remove the fruit from the liquid and place in a nonreactive bowl. Bring the liquid to a boil and continue cooking over high heat until reduced by half, about 15 minutes. The liquid will thicken when chilled. Pour the reduced liquid over the fruit. Stir in the liqueur. Refrigerate overnight.

Honey Poached Apricots

Makes about 3 cups; 6 servings

Poaching apricots is a quick and flavorful way to capture one of summer's greatest treats. If you are lucky enough to be invited to a summer barbecue, they make a wonderful hostess gift.

1 cup honey
¼ cup water
2 tablespoons fresh lemon juice
Zest of 1 lemon, in 1-inch strips
1 cinnamon stick
4 whole cloves
12 apricots

Note: To prevent the fruit from discoloring, submerge it fully in the poaching liquid. The fruit will keep refrigerated for about 1 week. Serve warm or chilled.

In a small, heavy nonreactive saucepan, combine the honey, water, lemon juice, lemon zest, cinnamon stick, and cloves and bring to a boil. In order not to crowd the pan, work with a few apricots at a time; halve the apricots and remove the pits. Drop the apricot halves into the liquid and cook just until tender, about 2 minutes. Remove with a slotted spoon and repeat until all the apricots are poached.

Let the poaching liquid cool. Place the apricots in a wide mouthed jar and cover with the poaching liquid and spices.

Fresh Figs with Orange Mascarpone Cream

Makes 6 servings

Unlike dried figs, I find the fresh fruit to be surprisingly light, making them the perfect foil to rich, creamy mascarpone.

12 fresh figs, cut into quarters
1¼ cups mascarpone cheese, at room temperature (see box)
1 tablespoon fresh orange juice
½ teaspoon pure vanilla extract
About 1 cup water
1 tablespoon orange zest

Divide the figs equally among 6 dessert bowls or glasses.

Using a whisk, beat the mascarpone with the orange juice and vanilla extract in a nonreactive bowl.

In a small saucepan, bring about 1 cup of water to a boil. Blanch the orange zest for 30 seconds; drain and chop finely. Fold the zest into the mascarpone. Spoon over the figs and serve immediately.

Note: Flower waters have been used since the Middle Ages. Orange blossom water is made from distilled orange blossoms; rose water is made from rose blossoms. Their flavors are intense, so use them sparingly. It is best to add them in advance so the flavor can blend with the other ingredients. Flower waters are available in stores specializing in Middle Eastern foods.

Orange Blossom–Scented Fruit Salad

Makes 4 servings

The exotic fragrant flavor of this refreshing fruit salad has its origins in Spain. For a great presentation, make it in a beautifully decorated bowl for a tapas buffet.

⅓ **cup sliced almonds**
4 **large navel oranges**
1 **large pink grapefruit**
3 **tablespoons orange blossom water (see Note)**
2 **tablespoons honey**
2 **teaspoons fresh lemon juice**

Preheat the oven to 325°F. Spread the almonds onto a baking sheet and toast until golden, about 5 minutes. Let them cool. Have ready a 4- to 6-cup decorative bowl.

Peel the oranges and the grapefruit over a bowl to catch any juice, making sure to remove all the pith. Cut the fruit crosswise into thin slices, about ¼-inch thick. Begin by placing a layer of the orange slices in the bottom of the decorative bowl. Sprinkle one-third of the toasted almonds on top of the oranges slices. Layer the grapefruit slices on top of the almonds, and sprinkle with more almonds. Repeat with the remaining oranges, finishing with a sprinkle of the almonds.

In the bowl containing the fruit juice, mix together the orange blossom water, honey, and lemon juice. Pour the liquid mixture over the fruit and cover the bowl with plastic wrap. Let the fruit sit in the refrigerator for at least 2 hours or overnight before serving.

To serve, present the bowl at the table and spoon into individual bowls.

Peach-Raspberry Cobbler

Makes 6 servings

A cobbler is basically a mixture of fruit topped with a sweet biscuit dough. It is important not to overcook the topping while making sure the fruit is thoroughly cooked. My friend Evelyn Patterson accomplishes this by cooking the fruit first. Remember, the fruit will need to come to a boil in the oven in order for the bottom of the biscuits to be cooked. Peaches work well with this method. Here they have been teamed with raspberries, but any berry or cherry can play.

Fruit filling

8 ripe peaches, peeled and sliced

⅓ cup Sucanat, or to taste

1 cup raspberries

½ teaspoon ground cinnamon

1 teaspoon lemon zest, finely chopped

1 tablespoon cornstarch

About 2 tablespoons water

1 tablespoon unsalted butter

Topping

1½ cups unbleached all-purpose flour

2 tablespoons maple sugar

1 teaspoon baking powder

½ teaspoon baking soda

½ teaspoon salt

¼ cup (½ stick) unsalted butter, chilled

⅔ cup buttermilk

Preheat the oven to 400°F. Have ready one 8 × 2-inch-round glass baking dish.

In a large nonreactive saucepan, combine the peaches with the Sucanat and cook over medium heat, stirring often, just until tender. Taste the juice for sweetness and add more Sucanat if desired. If more is added, cook until the sweetener is dissolved. Remove from the heat and stir in the berries, cinnamon, and zest.

In a small bowl, dissolve the cornstarch in about 2 tablespoons water to make a runny, smooth mixture and stir into the fruit. Return to the heat and bring to a boil. Remove from the heat and stir in the butter. Transfer to the baking dish.

To prepare the topping, combine the flour, maple sugar, baking powder, baking soda, and salt in the bowl of a food processor fitted with the steel blade. To blend the ingredients, turn the processor on and off, pulsing 3 to 5 times for a few seconds each time.

Cut the butter into 1-inch cubes. Uncover the bowl of the processor and put the butter on top of the dry ingredients, distributing it evenly. To cut the butter into the flour mixture, replace the cover, and using a pulsing action again, turn the machine on and off 8 to 10 times. Continue just until it resembles a coarse meal. Do not over process. If the butter begins to melt, refrigerate until firm.

Turn the mixture into a large mixing bowl. Pour in the buttermilk. Using a fork, blend the ingredients to absorb the liquid. At this point the ingredients may look very dry. Use your hands to press the mixture together.

On a lightly floured surface, roll the dough into a ¾-inch-thick disk. Use a 2-inch-round biscuit cutter or small glass to cut out as many biscuits as needed to cover the top of the baking dish, about 13, rerolling scraps, if necessary. Bake for 20 to 25 minutes, or until the fruit is bubbling and the biscuits are thoroughly cooked and their tops are lightly browned.

Pineapple Compote

Makes about 5 cups; 6 servings

Pineapple provides a fresh addition to a traditional compote. Choose a super-sweet pineapple for best results.

- **1 fresh pineapple, peeled and cored**
- **20 large prunes, pitted**
- **15 dried apricots**
- **¼ cup fresh orange juice**
- **½ cup water**
- **¼ cup Sucanat**
- **1 cinnamon stick**
- **2 tablespoons orange-flavored liqueur (Grand Marnier), (optional)**

Remove all the peel and spiky bits from the pineapple and cut the flesh into large chunks. In a medium nonreactive saucepan, combine the pineapple, prunes, apricots, orange juice, water, Sucanat, and cinnamon stick. Cook over medium heat until the mixture comes to a boil. Reduce the heat to low and cook the mixture until the fruit has softened and most of the liquid has reduced, about 30 minutes. Stir in the orange liqueur, if desired. Serve warm or chilled.

Poached Apples with Orange and Cardamom

Makes 6 servings

I once had a job preparing lunch for a Senior Citizens' Social Club. One of the volunteers, Khorshed, is a wonderful cook, and offered to teach me about East Indian food. On Friday mornings I would arrive at her apartment, which was across the street from where the club met, to help her prepare a five-course lunch, while learning new ways to use an array of spices in both savory and sweet dishes. The greatest lesson I learned was that for many of these spices, less is more.

As this dish cooks, the uniqueness of the spices will come alive. As in any great dish, you want every part to be important to the whole. Just a few cardamom seeds will flavor the whole dessert. Here, the apples become infused with the flavors of orange and spice. If you plan to serve the apples sliced, you may want to cut them in half and core them before poaching.

This recipe calls for wine, which in addition to providing flavor, helps to preserve the fruit. If you choose to leave it out, just add more citrus juice.

> 2½ cups water
> 1 cup honey
> 1 orange
> 1 tablespoon freshly squeezed lemon juice
> 1 cinnamon stick
> 1 whole clove
> Seeds from 1 green cardamom pod
> 6 apples (see box, page 153)

In a large nonreactive saucepan, combine the water and honey. Use a vegetable peeler to remove the zest from the orange, trying not to remove the white pith. Add to the liquid mixture. With a strainer set over the saucepan, squeeze the juice from the orange into the poaching liquid.

Add the lemon juice. Add the cinnamon stick, clove, and cardamom seeds. Cook the liquid over medium-low heat until it begins to simmer, about 15 minutes.

To prevent the apples from discoloring, drop each apple gently into the simmering liquid as it is peeled and cored. Make sure the fruit is submerged in the poaching liquid, turning the fruit, if necessary. Cook until the fruit is tender, 15 to 20 minutes. Test for doneness by gently inserting a skewer into the fruit.

Remove from the heat and let the fruit steep in the liquid for at least 3 hours. Remove the cinnamon stick. It is best to leave the fruit in the liquid overnight.

To reduce the liquid, remove the fruit. Strain the liquid and discard the flavorings. In a nonreactive saucepan, bring the liquid to a rapid boil over high heat. Continue cooking until the mixture has reduced by half, about 30 minutes. You should have about 1 cup of golden liquid. Serve the fruit at any desired temperature—warmed, chilled, or room temperature—with the reduced poaching liquid, or reserve the sauce to pour over ice cream. Or, better yet, serve the apples with the ice cream and the golden liquid.

Poached Pears with Fresh Ginger and Wine

Makes 4 servings

For some reason, when the term "poached" is used, it conjures up something far more sophisticated than if using the term "cooked." Ironically, poaching is a method that is quicker to do than many other techniques, yet produces highly flavored results. When poaching fruit, select fruit that is ripe and firm without any blemishes. The fruit becomes infused with the poaching liquid. Most recipes call for wine; in addition to the flavor, the acidity helps to preserve the fruit. If you choose to leave it out, just add a little more citrus juice.

2 cups water
½ cup white wine (optional)
¾ cup honey
1 lemon
½-inch piece fresh ginger
1 whole clove
4 to 6 ripe Anjou pears

In a large nonreactive saucepan, combine the water, wine, if desired, and honey. Using a vegetable peeler, remove the zest from the lemon trying not to remove the white pith. Add to the liquid mixture. With a strainer set over the saucepan, squeeze the juice from the lemon into the poaching liquid.

Thinly slice the ginger into 4 pieces and add to the liquid. Add the clove. Cook the liquid over medium-low heat until it begins to simmer. Cook for about 15 minutes.

To prevent the pears from discoloring, drop each pear gently into the simmering liquid as it is peeled. If the pears will be served sliced, you may want to cut them in half and core them before poaching. Make sure the fruit is submerged in the poaching liquid, turning the fruit, if necessary. Cook until the fruit is tender. Test for doneness by gently inserting a skewer into the fruit.

Remove from the heat and let the fruit steep in the liquid for at least 3 hours. It is best to leave the fruit in the liquid overnight.

To reduce the liquid, remove the fruit. Strain the liquid and discard the flavorings. In a nonreactive saucepan, bring the liquid to a rapid boil over high heat. Continue cooking until the mixture has reduced by half, about 30 minutes. You should have about 1 cup of golden liquid remaining. Serve the fruit at any desired temperature—warmed, chilled, or room temperature—with the reduced poaching liquid. You can also pour the sauce over ice cream or serve with the Pear Ginger Strudel on page 172.

Roasted Apricots

Makes 4 servings

Roasting has always been one of my favorite ways to bring out the flavor of meats and vegetables, so why not do it with fruit? The short roasting time fruit requires is an added bonus.

2 tablespoons unsalted butter
⅓ cup Sucanat
2 tablespoons water
½ teaspoon pure vanilla extract
1 tablespoon orange-flavored liqueur (Grand Marnier)
8 apricots, cut in half and pitted
1 cup whipped cream (optional, see box, page 68)

Preheat the oven to 375°F.

In a 9 × 13-inch glass baking dish, combine the butter, Sucanat, and water. Bake until the Sucanat has dissolved and begins to boil, about 8 minutes. Remove from the oven and stir in the vanilla extract and the liqueur. Place the apricots cut side down and return to the oven. Bake just until the fruit is tender, about 10 minutes.

Serve warm. Place 4 halves on each plate, cut side up. Spoon the sauce over the fruit and add a dollop of whipped cream, if desired.

Chapter Four

CAKES

*W*e have all heard the phrase "It's a piece of cake." But as most bakers can attest, there is quite a large range of difficulty involved in producing that "piece." Cakes can be either simple or elaborate, depending on how many components are required to complete them. These cake recipes have been selected to provide you with both a range of difficulty and a variety of tastes and textures.

I have always believed that no matter what the finishing touches are, a great cake should be able to stand alone. Even when I have suggested icings or accompanying sauces, don't be afraid to serve these cakes with a simple dollop of whipped cream or a good cup of coffee! When you decide to prepare one of the more elaborate cakes, remember that the cake, and most of the sauces, can be prepared in advance.

The natural sweeteners used in the preparation of these cakes may initially require you to change your visual expectations. Since white sugar is not called for, you will not produce a snow-white cake; however, you will create delicious, mouthwatering cakes and tortes.

Here are some general rules for successful cake baking: First, have ingredients such as eggs and milk at room temperature. Second, use the correct size pan. In most cases, you will be able to divide a batter into smaller pans, which requires you to reduce the baking time. However, when a recipe calls for two pans, baking it in one large pan may not work. The batter may be too heavy and require additional baking time, causing the corners to become overbaked while you try to get the center to cook. Finally, bake the cakes on a center rack of the oven, if not otherwise specified. With this in mind, this chapter really is a piece of cake!

Almond Torte

Makes one 2-layer cake; 8 servings

Use either almond- or orange-flavored liqueur to make this buttery nut torte. Simply layering it with your favorite flavor of all-fruit spread and decorating it with toasted almonds completes the delicious experience.

1½ cups whole raw almonds

1 cup maple sugar

¼ cup cornstarch

¼ cup unbleached all-purpose flour

1 teaspoon baking powder

¼ teaspoon salt

6 large eggs

¼ cup almond-flavored liqueur

10 tablespoons (1¼ sticks) unsalted butter, melted and cooled to room temperature

1 cup blackberry all-fruit spread, plus more for decorating

¼ cup toasted sliced almonds

Preheat the oven to 375°F. Butter two 8-inch-round cake pans. Have ready a wire rack covered with parchment paper. Pierce the paper with the tines of a fork to allow the steam to escape.

In the bowl of a food processor fitted with the steel blade, combine the whole almonds and maple sugar. Process until finely ground. In a separate bowl, sift together the cornstarch, flour, baking powder, and salt; set aside.

Transfer the nut mixture to the large bowl of an electric mixer. Add 2 eggs and beat on low speed until blended, about 1 minute. Add the remaining eggs 1 at a time, beating on high speed for 4 minutes after each addition. The egg mixture should become lighter in color and increase in volume.

Beat in the liqueur. Sprinkle the flour mixture over the egg mixture; fold in using a large rubber spatula until blended. Fold in the melted butter making sure to scrape the bottom as you fold; the butter has a tendency to sink, giving the appearance of being blended when it is not. Gently pour the batter into the prepared pans.

Bake for 15 minutes. Reduce the heat to 350°F. Continue baking for about 10 minutes or until a cake tester inserted into the center comes out clean. Remove from the oven and immediately loosen the sides of the torte with a knife. Invert the cakes onto the wire rack prepared with the parchment paper. The tortes should release from the pans to expose a flat, nutty bottom. Cool completely.

In a small nonreactive saucepan, melt the fruit spread over low heat. Keeping the torte upside down, spread the fruit spread over one layer, reserving a little for decorating; top with the second layer, flipping it so the bottom is on top. To create a decorative finish, spoon a thin line of the reserved fruit spread along the edge of the torte. Using the fruit spread as glue, sprinkle the toasted sliced almonds along the edge.

Apple Orange Caramel Cake

Makes 12 servings

We are fortunate, some would agree, to live in an era when geographic location does not have to dictate seasonal choices in food. This cake demonstrates the complex variety of winter's bounty. Sweet northern apples and refreshing southern oranges are topped off with an everyday decadence—caramel!

Cake

    4 apples, peeled and cored (see box, page 153)

    2 cups maple sugar or Sucanat

    4 teaspoons ground cinnamon

    1 cup vegetable oil

    ¼ cup freshly squeezed orange juice

    4 large eggs

    1 teaspoon orange zest, finely chopped

    1 tablespoon pure vanilla extract

    3 cups unbleached all-purpose flour

    1 tablespoon baking powder

    1 teaspoon salt

Glaze

    ½ cup (1 stick) unsalted butter

    ½ cup maple syrup

    ¼ cup heavy cream

Preheat the oven to 375°F. Butter one 9 × 12-inch baking pan.

Slice apples into ¼-inch-thick wedges and toss them with ¼ cup of the maple sugar and the cinnamon in a nonreactive bowl. Set aside.

In a large bowl, combine the oil, juice, eggs, zest, and vanilla extract.

In another large bowl, sift together the flour, the remaining maple sugar, baking powder, and salt. Add to the liquid mixture and blend together to form a thick batter.

Pour half of the batter into the baking pan and spread to cover the bottom. Arrange the apple slices in rows on the batter. Cover with the remaining batter. Bake for 45 minutes to 1 hour, or until a cake tester inserted into the center comes out clean. Remove from the oven and make holes in the top using a cake tester. Glaze while still warm.

To make the glaze, combine the butter, maple syrup, and cream in a small saucepan and bring to a boil over medium-high heat. Continue cooking until the butter no longer separates from the syrup and the glaze is smooth, about 8 minutes. Leave the warm cake in the pan and pour the glaze over it.

Apricot Crumb Cake

Makes 1 cake; 8 servings

Crumb cake reminds me of my childhood and of small European-style bakeries where my mother would buy a "nice" rye bread with caraway seeds. Crumb cakes may be a little old-fashioned, but they can still be quite a delicious way to bake fresh fruit.

Cake

- ½ cup (1 stick) unsalted butter, at room temperature
- ⅔ cup maple sugar
- 1 large egg
- 3 large egg yolks
- 1 teaspoon lemon zest, finely chopped
- 1 teaspoon pure vanilla extract
- 1½ cups unbleached all-purpose flour
- 1 teaspoon baking powder
- Pinch of salt
- 10 ripe medium apricots, washed

Crumb topping

- 1⅓ cups unbleached all-purpose flour
- ⅓ cup maple sugar
- ½ teaspoon ground cinnamon
- ½ cup (1 stick) unsalted butter, melted

Preheat the oven to 350°F. Butter one 10-inch-round tart pan with a removable bottom.

In the bowl of an electric mixer, cream the butter at medium speed for 1 minute. Gradually beat in the maple sugar. Cream the butter and sugar until light and fluffy, about 5 minutes. Beat in the egg. Add the egg yolks one at a time, beating well after each addition. Beat in the lemon zest and vanilla extract.

In a large bowl, sift together the flour, baking powder, and salt. Using a wooden spoon, stir the dry ingredients into the creamed mixture. Spoon the soft batter into the tart pan and use a spatula to level the batter.

Cut the apricots in half and remove the pits. Place each half cut side down on top of the batter, leaving a little space between each.

To make the crumb topping, in a separate medium bowl combine the flour, maple sugar, and cinnamon. Pour in the melted butter. Using either a wooden spoon or your hands, rub the ingredients together to form crumbs. Sprinkle the crumbs over and in between the fruit. Bake for about 55 minutes or until the center of the cake is no longer liquid or tester comes out clean. Let the cake cool before serving.

Note: After baking about 30 minutes, the top will become lightly browned. To prevent it from becoming too brown, place a piece of aluminum foil over the cake. Pierce the foil with a fork to allow the steam to escape and continue baking as directed.

Aunt Josephine's Chocolate Cake

Makes 1 cake; 10 servings

Aunt Josephine has been best friends with my mother for more than 50 years, and even though this is the only chocolate cake my mother has ever made, the name has never changed. I have even had new catering clients ask for it by name.

If you prefer your chocolate cake to have a rich, dense texture, this recipe may also become the only chocolate cake you will ever make!

I prefer to dust the cake with cocoa powder and serve it with whipped cream and fresh strawberries, but that is not to say you won't want to make it even richer by finishing it with a buttercream frosting. In either case, no one will believe how quick it is to make or how pleasing it can be to eat.

1 cup water

½ cup (1 stick) unsalted butter

4 ounces unsweetened chocolate

1 teaspoon baking soda

1 cup sour cream or plain yogurt

2 cups maple sugar

2 cups unbleached all-purpose flour

Pinch of salt

2 large eggs, beaten

1 teaspoon pure vanilla extract

Preheat the oven to 350°F. Butter one 12 × 8-inch ovenproof baking dish or two 9-inch-round cake pans.

In a small saucepan, bring the water and the butter to a boil over medium-high heat. Remove from the heat and add the chocolate. Stir until melted. Let cool while you prepare the other ingredients.

In a small nonreactive bowl, stir the baking soda into the sour cream and set aside.

In a large bowl, mix together the maple sugar, flour, and salt.

Into the chocolate mixture, while stirring with a whisk, pour in the beaten eggs. Blend thoroughly. Pour the chocolate–egg mixture into the dry ingredients and stir until incorporated. Stir in the vanilla and sour cream mixture.

Pour the batter into the prepared baking pan(s). Bake for about 35 minutes if using only 1 pan. Bake about 25 minutes if using 2 pans. The cake is done when a cake tester inserted in the center comes out clean. Let the cake cool in the pan. This cake will keep up to 4 days in the refrigerator or it may be frozen for up to 3 weeks if wrapped well. Serve at room temperature either frosted or dusted with cocoa.

Sweet Notes

Maple sugar granules are larger than refined sugar. Sometimes the larger granules do not melt well during baking, causing the top of the cake to crack. This cracked surface will not affect the flavor of the cake, but if you want a perfect-looking cake, it is best to start by making the maple sugar finer by grinding it in a food processor fitted with the steel blade. Process it for 2 to 3 minutes.

For a presentation requiring a perfectly even surface, use the bottom of the cake as the top. Level off the cracked top and turn the cake upside-down. Dust with cocoa. No one will ever know.

Whipping Cream

Although North Americans are trying to limit the amount of fat they consume, we all know that sometimes there is no substitute for the real thing. A dollop of real whipped cream can turn a plain piece of cake into an elegant dessert.

For best results, chill the bowl and beaters. You can add a little pure vanilla extract or a flavored liqueur, and depending on your taste, the cream can be sweetened with a few teaspoons of honey or maple syrup.

Pour the cream into the chilled bowl and beat at high speed just until soft peaks form. Watch carefully, making sure the beaters come in contact with all of the cream. For a firmer consistency, turn the machine on and off to check for firmness. There is a very short time difference between soft peaks and firm peaks. (Once you have firm peaks, there is even a shorter time between whipped cream and butter.)

Whipped cream has a tendency to separate when made in advance. If you do not want to beat it at the last minute, prepare it 2 or 3 hours in advance and place it in a fine strainer set over a bowl, cover with plastic wrap, and refrigerate.

Berry Hazelnut Crumb Cake

Makes 8 servings

Sweet, juicy berries are a sure indication it's really summer. This recipe requires the same preparation as the Apricot Crumb Cake (page 64) only with the addition of hazelnuts, which gives another dimension of flavor and a crunch to the crumb.

requires the same preparation as the Apricot Crumb Cake (page 64) only

Cake

½ cup (1 stick) unsalted butter, at room temperature
⅔ cup maple sugar
1 large egg
3 large egg yolks
2 teaspoons lemon zest, finely chopped
1 teaspoon pure vanilla extract
1½ cups unbleached all-purpose flour
1 teaspoon baking powder
Pinch of salt
2 cups fresh blueberries, rinsed and stemmed
1 cup fresh raspberries
½ teaspoon ground cinnamon

Crumb topping

1 cup unbleached all-purpose flour
⅓ cup maple sugar
½ cup sliced hazelnuts
¼ teaspoon ground cinnamon
½ cup (1 stick) unsalted butter, melted

Preheat the oven to 350°F. Butter a 10-inch-round tart pan with a removable bottom.

In the bowl of an electric mixer, cream the butter at medium speed for 1 minute. Gradually beat in the maple sugar. Cream the butter and sugar until it is light and fluffy, about 5 minutes. Beat in the egg. Add the egg yolks one at a time, beating well after each addition. Beat in 1 teaspoon of the lemon zest and the vanilla extract.

Note: After baking about 30 minutes, the top will become lightly browned. To prevent it from becoming too brown, place a piece of aluminum foil over the cake. Pierce the foil with a fork to allow the steam to escape and continue baking as directed.

In a large bowl, sift together the flour, baking powder, and salt. Using a wooden spoon, stir the dry ingredients into the creamed mixture. Spoon the soft batter into the tart pan and use a spatula to level the batter.

In a separate bowl, combine the berries with the reserved lemon zest and the cinnamon. Gently spread the berries over the batter, leaving a little space here and there.

To make the crumb topping, in a clean medium bowl, combine the flour, maple sugar, hazelnuts, and cinnamon. Pour in the melted butter. Using either a wooden spoon or your hands, rub the ingredients together to form crumbs. Sprinkle the crumbs over and in between the fruit.

Bake for about 55 minutes, until the center of the cake is no longer liquid, or the cake tester comes out clean. Let the cake cool before serving.

Black Plum Kuchen

Makes 12 servings

Black plums have always been my sister's favorite fruit. They seem to have more substance than the smaller plum varieties, but just as much juice. Inspired by a Mennonite recipe, this dessert uses a two-step baking method to allow the juice to be absorbed by the crust while the sour cream topping locks in the flavor. Other juicy fruits such as berries or nectarines will also work. I try to select fruit that doesn't require any peeling.

Fruit layer

6 to 8 ripe black plums

1 teaspoon ground cinnamon

¼ cup granular FruitSource (see Note), plus 2 tablespoons for additional sweetening

Crust

1½ cups unbleached all-purpose

¼ cup granular FruitSource

¼ teaspoon baking powder

¼ teaspoon salt

½ cup (1 stick) unsalted butter, chilled

Topping

1 cup sour cream

1 large egg

2 tablespoons brown rice syrup

½ teaspoon pure vanilla extract

Preheat the oven to 350°F. Butter one 8 × 12-inch glass baking dish.

Remove the pits from the plums and cut the fruit into 3 or 4 circles. Place in a large nonreactive mixing bowl. Sprinkle with the cinnamon and the ¼ cup of FruitSource. Set aside.

To make the crust, combine the flour, FruitSource, baking powder, and salt in the bowl of a food processor fitted with the steel blade. Process for a few seconds. Cut the butter into chunks and add to the dry ingredients. Turn the machine on and off in a pulsing action until the mixture resembles fine meal, about 8 times.

Transfer the mixture to the baking dish and press down. Arrange the plum slices evenly on top. Pour any juice from the bowl over the fruit and sprinkle with the remaining 2 tablespoons of FruitSource. Bake in the oven for 15 minutes. The juice should bubble.

Meanwhile, in a small nonreactive bowl, blend the sour cream, egg, brown rice syrup, and vanilla extract. Pour over the partially cooked fruit and continue to bake for 20 to 30 minutes, or until the juice is bubbling and the topping is set. Serve chilled or at room temperature.

Note:
itSource is a it-and-grain weetener that comes in both liquid and nular forms. e granules do not dissolve easily when creamed with utter, but the eetener works ll for specific recipes that ave more of a shortbread sistency. For where to buy itSource, see Source List, page 235.

Coconut-Strawberry Shortcake

Makes 8 shortcakes

There is nothing quite so delicious as ripe local strawberries. Their intense ruby color is matched only by their sweet taste. If you are lucky enough to be able to go to a strawberry farm and pick the berries yourself, you know it can take quite a bit of time to fill a quart, especially when two out of every three berries end up in your mouth. I have suggested that you sweeten the berries according to taste. If you are using local berries, adding sweetener may be unnecessary.

Shortcakes

3 cups unbleached all-purpose flour

4 teaspoons baking powder

1 teaspoon baking soda

½ teaspoon salt

½ cup (1 stick) unsalted butter, chilled

⅔ cup shredded unsweetened coconut

1 cup buttermilk

¼ cup honey

2 large eggs

1 teaspoon pure vanilla extract

Glaze

1 large egg yolk

1 teaspoon water

½ cup shredded unsweetened coconut

Garnish

4 cups strawberries

Juice of ¼ of a lemon (optional)

2 cups heavy cream

1 teaspoon pure vanilla extract

2 teaspoons honey or maple syrup

Preheat the oven to 400°F. Line a large baking sheet with parchment paper.

In a large bowl, sift together the flour, baking powder, baking soda, and salt. Cut the butter into the flour until it resembles coarse meal. This may be done either by hand using a pastry cutter or with a food processor. If using the food processor, put the ingredients into the bowl fitted with the steel blade and pulse the machine on and off, about 10 times. Transfer the ingredients into the large bowl. Mix in the coconut.

In a separate medium bowl, mix the buttermilk, honey, eggs, and vanilla extract until thoroughly blended. Add the liquid mixture to the dry ingredients. Using a fork, combine the ingredients, allowing the flour to absorb the moisture from the wet ingredients.

Use your hands to gently knead the dough 3 to 4 times, just until it holds together. Turn the dough onto a lightly floured work surface. Sprinkle the top of the dough very lightly with flour and roll out until it is 1½ inches thick. Use a 3-inch-round biscuit cutter to make 8 biscuits. Place them on the prepared cookie sheet.

To make the egg glaze, use a fork to combine the egg yolk with the water in a small bowl. Brush the tops of the biscuits with the glaze. Sprinkle the shredded coconut on top of the egg glaze. Bake for about 18 minutes or until the bottoms are lightly browned and the centers are baked. Cool on a wire rack.

Wash and hull the strawberries. Cut the small berries in half and slice the larger ones into multiple pieces. If desired, toss the berries with the lemon juice and sweeten to taste.

In a chilled large bowl, combine the cream, vanilla extract, and sweetener. Whip either by hand or with an electric mixer until soft peaks form (see box, page 68).

To assemble the desserts, split each shortcake in half crosswise. Spoon the berries on the bottom half of the shortcake, letting the cake absorb some of the juice. Spoon the whipped cream on top of the berries and cover with the top half of the shortcake. Serve immediately.

Cornmeal Cake with Honey-Rosemary Syrup and Raspberries

Makes 1 cake; 8 servings

Although people usually associate rosemary with savory dishes, its fragrant taste lends itself to sweet combinations. This is a light cornmeal cake infused with a sweet rosemary-flavored syrup. Add a scoop of mascarpone and some juicy fresh berries to create a surprise finish to a great summertime meal.

Cake

½ cup (1 stick) unsalted butter, at room temperature

½ cup maple syrup

1 cup yellow cornmeal

¾ cup unbleached all-purpose flour

1 teaspoon baking powder

½ teaspoon salt

2 large eggs

1 large egg yolk

⅔ cup milk

Syrup

¾ cup water

¾ cup honey

⅓ cup fresh rosemary leaves, chopped

1 tablespoon freshly squeezed lemon juice

½ teaspoon pure vanilla extract

To serve

1 cup mascarpone cheese (see box, page 50)

1 pint fresh raspberries

Preheat the oven to 350°F. Butter an 8 × 2-inch-round cake pan.

In the large bowl of an electric mixer, cream the butter and maple syrup until light, about 2 minutes. In separate medium bowl, sift together the cornmeal, flour, baking powder, and salt.

To the butter mixture, add the sifted ingredients, eggs, egg yolk, and milk and mix on low speed to combine. Turn the mixer on medium-high and beat until the batter is light yellow and fluffy, about 3 minutes.

Pour the batter into the prepared pan and use a spatula to level the top. Bake for 30 to 40 minutes, or until a cake tester inserted into the center comes out clean. Remove the cake from the oven and let it cool for 10 minutes in the pan. Loosen the sides and invert the cake onto a wire rack.

While the cake is baking, prepare the syrup. In a small nonreactive saucepan, combine the water, honey, rosemary, and lemon juice. Bring the syrup to a boil and cook for 10 minutes. Remove the syrup from the heat. Add the vanilla extract and let the rosemary continue to steep while it cools for 30 minutes.

Pour the syrup through a strainer set over a bowl. Brush one-third of the syrup over the warm cake. Refrigerate the remaining syrup until ready to serve. When the cake is completely cooled, wrap it in plastic wrap and leave it at room temperature overnight before serving.

To serve, slice the cake into 8 wedges. Divide the mascarpone cheese and the berries among the slices and spoon the remaining syrup onto the fruit.

Devil's Food Cake with Italian Meringue Chocolate Buttercream

Makes 1 double layer cake; 10 servings

This cake is just right for people who like a moist, but light textured, dark chocolate cake. For an elegant finish, serve the cake with Dark Chocolate Sauce (page 218).

Cake

1¾ cups all-purpose flour

¾ cup unsweetened cocoa powder, sifted

2 teaspoons baking soda

1 teaspoon baking powder

¼ teaspoon salt

1¾ cups maple sugar

1 cup buttermilk

1 cup strong coffee, at room temperature

½ cup vegetable oil

2 large eggs

Icing

1 batch Italian Meringue Chocolate Buttercream (page 224)

Position the rack in the center of the oven. Preheat the oven to 350°F. Butter two 9 × 1½-inch-round cake pans.

In a large bowl, sift together the flour, cocoa, baking soda, baking powder, and salt. Stir in the maple sugar.

In a medium bowl, beat together the buttermilk, coffee, vegetable oil, and eggs. Pour the liquid mixture into the dry ingredients and mix until the batter is smooth. Divide the batter evenly between the two pans.

Bake for about 25 minutes or until a cake tester inserted into the center of each cake comes out clean. Remove from the oven and let the cakes cool completely before icing.

Before icing, lightly brush the surface of each cake to remove any loose crumbs. Spread a layer of the buttercream over the top of one of the cake layers. Place the other layer on top. Spread the buttercream on top and over the sides of the entire cake. Decorate to your taste. Refrigerate until ready to serve. About 30 minutes prior to serving, remove the cake from the refrigerator to allow the buttercream to come to room temperature.

Hazelnut Blackberry Linzertorte

Makes 1 cake; 8 servings

Traditionally, linzertortes are made with almonds and raspberry jam, but I like the rich flavor of hazelnuts. You can use your favorite fruit spread.

Linzertorte

- 1⅓ cups unbleached all-purpose flour
- ⅓ cup granular FruitSource (see Note, page 235)
- 1 teaspoon baking powder
- ½ teaspoon ground cinnamon
- Pinch of salt
- 1 cup hazelnuts, skinned (see box, page 83) and finely ground
- 1 teaspoon lemon zest, finely chopped
- ¾ cup (1½ sticks) unsalted butter, at room temperature
- 1 large egg
- 1 large egg yolk
- 1 teaspoon pure vanilla extract
- ¾ cup blackberry all-fruit spread

Egg glaze

- 1 large egg yolk
- 1 teaspoon water
- ¼ cup sliced hazelnuts

Preheat the oven to 350°F. Butter one 9-inch-round cake pan.

In a large bowl, sift together the flour, FruitSource, baking powder, cinnamon, and salt. Stir in the ground hazelnuts and lemon zest. Either with your hands or with an electric mixer, blend the butter into the dry ingredients just until the mixture comes together.

In a small bowl, beat together the egg, egg yolk, and vanilla extract. Add the egg mixture to the batter and blend until a soft dough forms. Spread two-thirds of the dough into the prepared pan, pressing a ¼-inch–high edge of dough up the sides of the pan to help hold the jam. Spoon the jam onto the dough, making sure to stay within the raised edge and to prevent any dough showing through the layer of jam.

Divide the remaining one-third of the dough into 8 pieces. Dust your hands with flour and roll each piece between your hands to form logs. Flatten each log slightly and lay them over the jam to create the lattice top. Mix the egg yolk with water to make the glaze and brush it over the lattice top. Carefully sprinkle the sliced hazelnuts along the edge of the torte.

Bake for about 45 minutes or until the center is cooked (a cake tester inserted into the center comes out clean). To serve, slice into wedges.

Note: After baking about 30 minutes, the top will become lightly browned. To prevent it from becoming too brown, place a piece of aluminum foil over the torte. Pierce the foil with a fork to allow the steam to escape and continue baking as directed.

The Naturally Sweet Baker

Hazelnut Torte with Espresso Butter Cream

Makes 1 cake; 8 servings

A variation of the almond torte, this rich hazelnut torte has layers sandwiched between espresso-flavored French buttercream.

Torte

- 1½ cups sliced hazelnuts (see box, page 83)
- 1 cup maple sugar
- ¼ cup cornstarch
- ¼ cup unbleached all-purpose flour
- 1 teaspoon baking powder
- ¼ teaspoon salt
- 6 large eggs
- ¼ cup hazelnut-flavored liqueur (Frangelica)
- 10 tablespoons (1¼ sticks) unsalted butter, melted and cooled to room temperature

Icing

- 1 batch French Butter Cream (page 220)
- ½ cup toasted sliced hazelnuts (see box, page 83)

Preheat the oven to 375°F. Butter two 8-inch-round cake pans. Have ready a wire rack covered with parchment paper. Pierce the paper with the tines of a fork to allow the steam to escape.

In the bowl of a food processor fitted with the steel blade, combine the hazelnuts and maple sugar. Process until finely ground. In a separate small bowl, sift together the cornstarch, flour, baking powder, and salt and set aside.

Transfer the nut mixture to the large bowl of an electric mixer. Using an electric mixer, beat 2 eggs on low speed until blended, about 1 minute. Add the remaining eggs one at a time, beating at high speed for 4 minutes after each addition. The egg mixture should become lighter in color and increase in volume. Beat in the liqueur.

Sprinkle the flour mixture over the egg mixture and fold it in using a large rubber spatula, until blended. Fold in the melted butter, making sure to scrape the bottom as you fold. The butter has a tendency to sink, giving the appearance of being blended when it is not.

Gently pour the batter into the prepared pans. Bake for 15 minutes. Reduce the heat to 350°F. Continue baking for about 10 minutes or until a cake tester inserted into the center comes out clean. Remove the torte from the oven and immediately loosen the sides of each layer with a knife. Invert it onto the wire rack prepared with the parchment paper. The layers should release from the pan exposing a flat, nutty bottom. Cool completely.

Using a long, sharp serrated knife, slice each cake layer in half horizontally to create 4 even layers. Keeping the torte upside down, spread some buttercream over one layer; top with another layer of the torte and cover the top of that layer with some buttercream. Repeat the procedure, finishing with a layer of the torte cut side down. Spread buttercream over the top and sides of the torte. To create a decorative finish, sprinkle the sides with the sliced toasted hazelnuts. Keep refrigerated until about 30 minutes before serving.

Orange Layer Cake

Makes 1 cake; 8 servings

Layering a genoise with a fresh-tasting orange buttercream creates a very delicate cake that is perfect for any season or occasion. The buttercream may be piped for a special, more elaborate presentation or left plain for an understated elegance.

Imbibing syrup

3 tablespoons honey

⅓ cup hot water

⅓ cup cold water

3 tablespoons orange liqueur (Grand Marnier), or fresh orange juice

Cake

1 batch Genoise (page 222)

1 batch French Buttercream, flavored with orange liqueur, (page 220)

Imbibing syrup is a subtly liqueur- or fruit-flavored syrup that is sprinkled lightly on cakes to add additional flavor and moisture. To prepare the imbibing syrup for this recipe, in a small nonreactive bowl, dissolve the honey in the hot water. Mix in the cold water and orange liqueur.

Using a long, sharp serrated knife, slice each genoise cake layer in half horizontally to create 4 even layers. Lightly brush one layer of the cake with the imbibing syrup. Spread a thin layer of the buttercream over the cake layer. Repeat with the remaining layers. Finish the cake by spreading the buttercream over the top and sides.

Refrigerate the cake for at least 3 hours before serving. Allow the buttercream to come to room temperature by removing the cake from the refrigerator about 30 minutes before serving.

Lemon Cheesecake with Strawberry Rhubarb Sauce

Makes 1 cake; 10 servings

Health food products have come a long way over the years, especially in the cookie department. For this recipe I use prepared graham crackers, which are naturally sweetened and every bit as delicious as the ones I used to snack on as a kid.

This New York-style cheesecake has the fresh taste of lemon complemented with freshly grated nutmeg. Serve it with Strawberry Rhubarb Sauce (page 231).

Crust

1 cup graham cracker crumbs, about 10 crackers

⅓ cup unsalted butter, melted

½ teaspoon pure vanilla extract

Cheesecake filling

1½ pounds firm cream cheese, at room temperature

¼ cup honey

¼ cup apple juice concentrate

2 large eggs

1 tablespoon cornstarch

1 tablespoon freshly squeezed lemon juice

1 teaspoon pure vanilla extract

½ teaspoon freshly ground nutmeg

¾ cup sour cream

2 teaspoons lemon zest, finely chopped

Topping

1 batch Strawberry Rhubarb Sauce (page 231)

Preheat the oven to 350°F. Butter one 9-inch-round springform pan or one 9 × 2-inch fluted tart pan with a removable bottom.

To make the crust, use the above proportions, but follow the instructions for the Graham Cracker Crust on page 219. Place the crumb mixture into the pan. Use your hands to press the crumbs into an even layer. Bake for 5 minutes. Let cool. Increase the oven temperature to 375°F.

In the large bowl of an electric mixer, cream the cream cheese with the honey and apple juice concentrate. Beat in the eggs and cornstarch. Stir in the lemon juice and vanilla extract. Fold in the nutmeg, sour cream, and lemon zest.

Pour the filling into the crust and bake for 30 to 40 minutes, or until the sides are firm but the center is still soft. Be careful not to overbake the cake. To prevent cracking, when finished baking, turn off the oven and let the cake cool in the oven with the door ajar. Refrigerate overnight before serving. Serve with the Strawberry Rhubarb Sauce (page 231).

Toasting Hazelnuts

Toasting whole hazelnuts adds flavor and makes it possible to remove the skins. Always taste the nuts before toasting to make sure they are fresh.

Spread the whole nuts in a single layer onto a jellyroll pan, and bake at 325°F for 10 minutes (to loosen skins) or 20 minutes (to thoroughly toast the nuts). When toasted, transfer the nuts to a rough dish towel or apron and rub them to loosen the skins. Some skins will remain attached. Let nuts cool before proceeding with your recipe.

To toast sliced hazelnuts, spread a single layer onto a jellyroll pan and bake for 5 to 8 minutes at 325°F until golden brown. Watch them carefully so they do not burn.

Orange Poppy Seed Cake

Makes one 10-inch cake; 10 servings

The glaze keeps the cake moist while the poppy seeds create a traditional and fun crunch. If lemon is your pleasure, just substitute lemon zest for the orange zest and use ⅓ cup lemon juice and 3 tablespoons of orange juice in the glaze.

Cake

½ cup (1 stick) unsalted butter, at room temperature

¾ cup honey

4 large eggs

1 teaspoon pure vanilla extract

2 cups unbleached all-purpose flour

2 teaspoons baking soda

½ teaspoon salt

¾ cup buttermilk

⅓ cup poppy seeds

Zest of 2 oranges, finely chopped

Glaze

½ cup freshly squeezed orange juice

Juice of ½ lemon

¼ cup honey

Position the rack in the center of the oven. Preheat the oven to 350°F. Butter one 10-inch tube pan with a removable bottom.

In a large bowl of an electric mixer, cream the butter and honey together. Beat in the eggs one at a time, beating well after each addition. Beat in the vanilla extract. Transfer the butter mixture to the bowl of a food processor fitted with the steel blade. Process until the ingredients are emulsified, about 1 minute (see box, page 100). Return the cream mixture to the bowl.

In a separate large bowl, sift together the flour, baking soda, and salt. With the mixer on low speed, beat in one-third of the dry ingredients. Add half of the buttermilk. Continue alternating between

wet and dry until all of the ingredients have been added, ending with the dry ingredients. Fold in the poppy seeds and the orange zest.

Spoon the batter into the prepared tube pan. Bake for 40 to 45 minutes or until a cake tester inserted into the center comes out clean. Remove the cake from the oven and let cool for 5 minutes.

Meanwhile, to prepare the glaze, combine the orange and lemon juices and honey in a small nonreactive saucepan. Cook over medium heat until the mixture boils.

To enable the cake to absorb the glaze, make holes on the cake surface with a toothpick or skewer in several places. Brush the glaze over the warm cake making sure the glaze is allowed to go down the sides. Let the cake cool completely. This cake is best served the day after it is prepared. Keep in an airtight container until ready to serve.

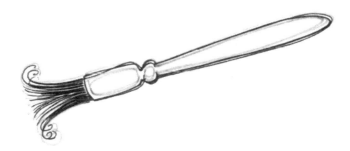

Rum and Raisin Ricotta Cake

Makes 1 cake; 12 servings

Whenever I'm buying fresh, creamy Ricotta cheese, I make sure to buy extra so I can have some as soon as I get home. If you have any left after you've had your snack, I suggest this crustless Ricotta cheesecake. Make sure to leave enough time for the raisins to soak up the rum, ensuring each bite will be filled with these plump, flavored morsels.

Raisins

- 1¼ cups organic Thompson dark raisins
- 1¼ cups golden raisins, preferably organic
- ¾ cup dark rum

Cake

- 2 pounds whole-milk Ricotta cheese, at room temperature
- ½ cup honey
- 6 large eggs, lightly beaten
- ¼ teaspoon salt
- 1 teaspoon ground cinnamon
- 1 teaspoon freshly ground nutmeg
- ⅓ cup unbleached all-purpose flour
- 2 teaspoons pure vanilla extract
- 2 teaspoons orange zest, finely chopped
- 2 teaspoons lemon zest, finely chopped

Topping

- 2 teaspoons cornstarch
- ½ cup apple juice, not from concentrate
- ½ teaspoon pure vanilla extract
- 2 tablespoons unsalted butter

In a medium nonreactive bowl, combine the raisins and rum. Cover with plastic wrap and let sit overnight.

Preheat the oven to 300°F. Butter and flour one 9-inch-round springform pan.

In a large bowl of an electric mixer, beat the Ricotta cheese on medium speed to lighten it, about 1 minute. Add the honey, eggs, salt, spices, and flour and continue beating until smooth. Fold in ½ cup of the soaked raisins, reserving the remainder for the topping. Fold in the vanilla extract and 1 teaspoon each of both types of zest.

Pour into the prepared pan. Bake for about 1 hour and 20 minutes, or until the cake is golden brown and the center is firm. Let cool and as it does so, the cake will deflate. When cool, remove from the springform pan and wrap in plastic wrap and refrigerate.

To prepare the topping, dissolve the cornstarch in about 2 tablespoons of the apple juice and set aside. In a small nonreactive saucepan, combine the reserved raisins, remaining apple juice, and vanilla extract. Cook over medium heat until the raisins plump up. Stirring constantly, pour in the cornstarch mixture and bring to boil; cook for 30 seconds. Remove from the heat; stir in the remaining zest and the butter. Spoon over the top of the chilled cake. To serve, slice into 12 wedges.

Spiced Prune and Rum Cake with Honey Lemon Cream Cheese Icing

Makes 1 cake; 12 servings

This wonderfully spiced cake gets much of its sweetness from the prunes. Serve it as a 4-layer cake or bake it in loaves. The smooth, creamy icing makes a great finish.

Cake

    30 unsulfured pitted prunes, quartered
    ½ cup dark rum
    1 cup (2 sticks) unsalted butter, at room temperature
    1½ cups maple sugar
    4 large eggs
    1 teaspoon pure vanilla extract
    3¼ cups unbleached all-purpose flour
    1 teaspoon baking soda
    2 teaspoons baking powder
    1 teaspoon ground cinnamon
    1 teaspoon ground cardamom
    ½ teaspoon ground nutmeg
    ½ teaspoon ground cloves
    ½ teaspoon salt
    1½ cups buttermilk

Icing

Honey Lemon Cream Cheese Icing (page 217)

In a medium saucepan, place the prunes and rum and add water to cover. Cook over medium heat until the prunes are soft and plump, about 20 minutes. Set aside.

Preheat the oven to 350°F. Butter two 9 × 9-inch baking pans.

In the large bowl of an electric mixer, cream together the butter and maple sugar on medium-high speed until light and fluffy. Add the eggs one at a time, beating thoroughly after each addition. Beat in the vanilla extract.

In a large bowl, sift together the flour, baking soda, baking powder, spices, and salt. Add the dry ingredients to the creamed mixture, alternating with the buttermilk, and finishing with the dry ingredients. Beat well after each addition, scraping down the bottom and sides of the bowl as necessary. Fold in the cooked prunes. Divide the batter equally between the two pans.

Bake for about 35 minutes or until a cake tester inserted in the center comes out clean. Let the cakes cool in the pans for 10 minutes before turning them out onto a wire rack to cool completely.

Cut each cake in half horizontally to create additional layers. Spread a layer of the icing over the top of one layer leaving the sides plain. Place a layer of cake on top of the first, repeating until all the layers are assembled. Finish by spreading a layer of icing over the top of the cake.

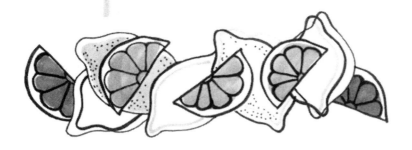

Upside-Down Pear Gingerbread with Caramel-Pear Sauce and Lemon Whipped Cream

Makes 1 cake; 10 servings

This recipe creates a playful, sophisticated, sensuous taste experience. The playfulness is achieved through what I call the "pineapple upside-down technique without the cherry." The senses are first sparked by the contrast in color between the glistening pears against the mahogany-colored cake. Then with one bite, the contrast between the flavor and texture of the pears with the fresh ginger and molasses comes into play. Finally, the warmth of the sweet caramel pear sauce combined with the coolness of the lemon whipped cream completes the sophisticated experience.

Caramel-Pear Sauce

1 cup maple syrup
½ cup honey
2 tablespoons unsalted butter
2 tablespoons pure vanilla extract

Gingerbread

5 ripe, firm Anjou pears
½ cup (1 stick) unsalted butter, at room temperature
½ cup maple sugar
2 large eggs
1 cup unsulfured molasses
¼ cup peeled fresh ginger, finely grated
1 cup unbleached all-purpose flour
1 cup whole-wheat flour
2 teaspoons baking soda
Pinch of salt
1 cup sour cream

Lemon Whipped Cream

1 cup heavy cream

2 teaspoons honey

½ teaspoon pure vanilla extract

1 teaspoon freshly squeezed lemon juice

1 teaspoon lemon zest, finely chopped

Preheat the oven to 350°F. Have ready one 10-inch-round nonstick baking pan.

To make the sauce: Combine the maple syrup, honey, and 2 tablespoons of butter in a small saucepan and bring to a boil over medium heat. Thicken the mixture by reducing it slightly. Remove from the heat and stir in the vanilla extract. Pour just enough syrup into the baking pan to coat the bottom, about ½ cup. Reserve the remaining syrup for serving with the cake.

To make the gingerbread: Peel and core 2 of the pears. Slice the pears into ¼-inch-thick wedges and put them into the pan to form an overlapping concentric circle. Reserve about 3 slices to use for the center of the circle. Cut the reserved slices in ½-inch pieces and fill in the circle.

In a the large bowl of an electric mixer, cream together the butter and maple sugar until light and fluffy. Add the eggs one at a time, beating well after each addition. Pour in the molasses and the ginger.

In a separate large bowl, sift together the flours, baking soda, and salt. Fold the dry ingredients into the creamed mixture alternating with the sour cream and ending with the dry ingredients. Pour the batter into the prepared pan.

Bake for about 45 minutes or until a cake tester inserted into the center of the cake comes out clean. Remove from the oven and let the cake rest for 3 minutes. To remove the cake from the pan, run a knife along its edges. Place a cake rack or plate over the cake and invert the pan with a little thrust to help to loosen the cake. If some of the pears stick to the pan, carefully remove them and reposition on the cake (no one has to know). Let the cake cool completely.

To finish the Caramel-Pear Sauce: Heat the reserved syrup over medium heat. Peel and core the remaining pears and slice them into ¼-inch-thick wedges. Cook the pears in the syrup until they are soft, but still firm. Keep warm until ready to serve.

To make the whipped cream: Combine the heavy cream, honey, and vanilla extract in a chilled medium bowl. Begin to beat the cream either by hand or with an electric mixer, and as the cream mounts add the lemon juice. Beat until soft peaks hold. Fold in the lemon zest.

To serve, slice the cake into 10 wedges. Place each wedge in the center of a dinner plate. Spoon some of the sauce to one side of the cake and some whipped cream to the other side of the cake. Enjoy!

The Naturally Sweet Baker

Chapter Five

COOKIES AND SQUARES

*S*maller than a piece of cake or pie, but just as big in flavor, cookies and squares can be a great snack or the perfect last bite to a delicious meal. They are often filled with fun tastes and many childhood memories. And best of all, they are portable sweets!

One of the most common characteristics of cookies is their crisp texture. When adapting classic and family recipes to be naturally sweet, I found preserving this characteristic to be a challenge, since the natural sweeteners are mostly liquid. It soon became clear that the use of maple sugar would produce cookies that were deliciously familiar. In most cases, maple sugar can be creamed with butter to replace white or brown sugar, requiring little or no other adjustments to standard recipes. When appropriate, liquid sweeteners have been used to create squares and cookies that are meant to be soft.

Another great cookie breakthrough came in the form of chocolate chips and other readily available selections of grain-sweetened, pure chocolate products. (The Source List on page 235 will provide more information to help you find suppliers in your area.) Add them to the square recipes or melt them to be used to garnish the desserts throughout the book.

Parchment paper provides the most effective nonstick surface you will find. It adds no extra calories and makes cleaning up a breeze. The cookies can be cooled on the paper and then easily transferred to a wire rack. In addition, parchment paper can be reused practically until it falls apart. Look for it in the supermarket and in specialty cookware shops.

I strongly recommend baking trays of cookies on only one rack at a time. If you use more than one rack, the cookies on the bottom tray bake only on the bottom, and only the tops of the cookies bake on the top tray. Needless to say, the cookies in the middle do not bake properly. If you have a wide oven, bake the trays side by side, on the same rack. Otherwise, use the single method and bake cookies on a center rack in the oven, unless other instructions are given. You will be rewarded for the extra time it takes through their evenly cooked appearance and their perfect taste.

Blood Orange Currant Cookies

Makes about 36 cookies

Some people cannot sleep if there is chocolate in the house, and my nights are restless when these cookies are around. A delicate, crispy, buttery cookie, these treats take on a unique color from the blood orange zest. If blood oranges are not in season, just substitute the zest of a navel orange.

Cookies

- **½ cup (1 stick) unsalted butter, at room temperature**
- **⅓ cup maple sugar**
- **1 large egg**
- **1 large egg yolk**
- **2 tablespoons ground almonds**
- **1⅔ cups unbleached all-purpose flour**
- **1 teaspoon baking powder**
- **½ cup dried organic currants**
- **Zest of 1 blood orange, finely chopped**

Egg glaze

- **1 large egg yolk, beaten**
- **1 teaspoon water**

To make the dough: Cream together the butter and maple sugar until light, either by hand or with an electric mixer in a medium bowl. Add the egg, egg yolk, and almonds and beat well, about 4 minutes.

In a medium bowl, sift together the flour and baking powder. Using a wooden spoon, mix the flour into the butter mixture just until incorporated. Add the currants and the zest and mix until blended. Wrap the dough in plastic and refrigerate for at least 1 hour.

Preheat the oven to 350°F. Butter 2 cookie sheets or line each with parchment paper.

On a lightly floured work surface, roll the dough out ⅛-inch thick. Cut into desired shapes, like diamonds, circles, or small hearts, and place cookies on the prepared baking sheets. The cookies can be placed close together because they will not spread when baked.

To make the egg glaze: In a small bowl, beat together the egg yolk and water and brush each cookie with this. Bake for about 13 minutes, or until the bottoms are lightly browned. Cool on a wire rack. The cookies will keep for about 1 week in an airtight container.

Butter Cookies

Makes 24 cookies

Some mothers bake shortbread—my mother baked her Aunt May's butter cookies. Even as a young girl, I always thought they were very sophisticated. As they bake, the dough spreads, just enough to make the centers like little butter cakes, while the edges are thin and crispy. My mother never used lemon zest, but I have included it. With or without it, they are delicious. Try them with the Grand Marnier–Caramel Gelato (page 143).

1 cup (2 sticks) unsalted butter, at room temperature

1 cup maple sugar

2 large eggs

2 teaspoons pure vanilla extract

1½ cups unbleached all-purpose flour

1 teaspoon orange or lemon zest, finely chopped (optional)

Preheat the oven to 325°F. Butter 2 cookie sheets or line each with parchment paper.

In the large bowl of an electric mixer, cream the butter and the sugar. Add the eggs and vanilla extract, beating until blended. Using a wooden spoon, stir in the flour and the zest, if desired.

To shape the cookies, drop by teaspoonfuls onto the prepared cookie sheets. Slightly flatten the centers of the cookies with your finger or the handle of a butter knife. Bake for about 10 minutes, or until the bottoms and the edges have browned. Transfer the cookies to a wire rack to cool. Store in an airtight container for up to three days or freeze for 2 weeks. Let the cookies come to room temperature before serving.

Cashew Butter Thumbprint Cookies

Makes about 48 cookies

Cashew butter is available in many health food stores. Its rich flavor has a more subtle taste than peanut butter. People will taste the difference between the two nut butters, but they won't be able to put their finger on it. Fill these cookies with your favorite all-fruit spreads.

1 cup (2 sticks) unsalted butter, at room temperature

1¼ cups maple sugar

1 large egg

¾ cup cashew butter

1 teaspoon pure vanilla extract

3½ cups unbleached all-purpose flour

½ teaspoon salt

¾ cup all-fruit spread

Preheat the oven to 350°F. Butter a cookie sheet or line it with parchment paper.

In the large bowl of an electric mixer, beat the butter for 30 seconds. Add the maple sugar and beat until creamy. Add the egg, cashew butter, and vanilla extract. Beat until well blended.

In a separate large bowl, sift together the flour and salt. Add the dry ingredients to the creamed mixture. Either by hand or using the electric mixer, blend all the ingredients together, just until combined (see Note).

To shape the cookies, roll 1 tablespoon of the dough between your palms to form a 1½-inch ball. Place the balls onto the cookie sheet and use your thumb to make an indentation in the center of each to hold the jam. Cover with plastic wrap and chill for at least 20 minutes. Just before baking, fill the centers with jam.

Bake for about 12 minutes or until the cookie bottoms are golden brown. Remove to a wire rack to cool. Store in an airtight container for up to 5 days.

Note: The dough can be prepared in advance and refrigerated overnight befo shaping.

Chocolate Brownie Espresso Chip Cookies

Makes 24 cookies

The only way to describe this recipe is to say that it is a combination of brownie and cookie. The maple syrup makes the cookies soft and cakey like a fudge brownie, and baking them on cookie sheets gives them a crisp bottom. Forget warm woolen mittens, these are a few of my favorite things!

1 cup (2 sticks) unsalted butter, at room temperature

1 cup maple syrup

2 large eggs

1 teaspoon pure vanilla extract

1½ cups unbleached all-purpose flour

1 cup cocoa

1 teaspoon baking soda

½ teaspoon salt

1½ cups naturally sweetened espresso chocolate chips (see Note)

Using the "new creaming technique" on page 100, cream the butter and the maple syrup. Add the eggs and vanilla extract. Process until light and fluffy. Transfer the mixture to a large mixing bowl.

In a medium bowl, sift together the flour, cocoa, baking soda, and salt. Using a wooden spoon, stir the dry ingredients into the creamed butter mixture. When just blended, mix in the chocolate chips. The mixture will be very soft. Cover with plastic wrap and refrigerate for at least 1 hour. (Mixture may be refrigerated overnight.)

Preheat the oven to 325°F. Butter two cookie sheets or line each with parchment paper.

Using a heaping tablespoon of dough for each cookie, place the dough in mounds 2 inches apart on the prepared cookie sheets. Bake one sheet at a time in the middle of the oven for about 12 minutes. The cookies are done when the centers have risen like little cakes. Remove and cool on cookie sheets for a minute before transferring to a wire rack.

Note: Tropical ce produces a e of naturally ened chocolate ducts: espresso iocolate chips, peanut butter iocolate chips, d a variety of olate bars that an be chopped ubstituted for the chips (see Source List, page 235).

A New Creaming Technique

I have found that the best way to cream together butter, liquid sweeteners such as honey or maple syrup, and eggs is to use a food processor fitted with the steel blade. The processor combines the ingredients more thoroughly than an electric mixer.

For best results, the butter and the eggs should be at room temperature and the liquid sweetener a little chilled. Begin by creaming the butter and liquid sweetener together in the work bowl of a food processor until both ingredients are thoroughly combined, 1 to 2 minutes. Add the eggs and process for another 1 to 2 minutes. Scrape down the sides of the work bowl as necessary. As air is incorporated into the mixture it will begin to resemble traditionally creamed ingredients, becoming light and fluffy. Once this is achieved, transfer the mixture to a mixing bowl and proceed with the recipe.

Chocolate Chip Cookies

Makes about 24 cookies

A classic. Maple sugar makes it possible to create a crispy yet moist cookie, and the availability of delicious, naturally sweetened, real chocolate chips will make these a staple in your cookie repertoire.

1 cup (2 sticks) unsalted butter, at room temperature
1½ cups maple sugar
2 large eggs
1 teaspoon pure vanilla extract
2½ cups unbleached all-purpose flour
1 teaspoon baking soda
½ teaspoon salt
2 cups semi-sweet grain-sweetened chocolate chips (see Note)

Preheat the oven to 325°F. Butter 2 cookie sheets or line each with parchment paper.

In the large bowl of an electric mixer, cream the butter and maple sugar, stopping to scrape down the sides of the bowl as necessary, until light and fluffy. Add the eggs and vanilla and continue to beat until the mixture is light and fluffy.

In a medium bowl, sift together the flour, baking soda, and salt. Using a wooden spoon, stir the dry ingredients into the creamed mixture, just until blended. Mix in chocolate chips.

Form cookies into mounds using a heaping tablespoonful of dough. Place the mounds 2 inches apart on the prepared cookie sheets. Bake one sheet at a time in the middle of the oven. For chewy cookies, bake for about 13 minutes, or until the centers have risen and the bottoms are golden brown. For crispier cookies, continue baking until the centers deflate, about 2 more minutes. Cool on the cookie sheet for a minute before using a large spatula to transfer them to a wire rack.

Note: Sunspire grain-sweetened chocolate and Tropical Source both produce pure chocolate, naturally sweetened chips. For where to buy grain-sweetened chocolate chips, see Source List (page 235).

Chocolate Shortbread

Makes 30 cookies

This is an adaptation of the best chocolate shortbread recipe I have ever found. The original recipe is the creation of Anna and Sybille Pump from their terrific book, The Loaves and Fishes Party Cookbook. *I have received raves whenever I have made them according to the original recipe, which produces a rich, bittersweet cookie.*

My only concern about adapting the recipe for this book was that the original recipe calls for confectioner's sugar, which is powdery and much finer than any of the granular natural sweeteners. My solution was to grind the maple sugar in a food processor before adding the other ingredients. This technique produced a dough slightly more granular in texture, but a cookie that was every bit as delicious as the original. Cut them in different shapes, depending on the occasion.

1¼ cups maple sugar

2 cups unbleached all-purpose flour

¾ cup cocoa powder

1 teaspoon pure vanilla extract

9 ounces (2¼ sticks) cold unsalted butter, cut into small pieces

Place the maple sugar in the bowl of a food processor fitted with the steel blade. Process for 2 minutes. The sugar will become somewhat finer but not powdery.

Add the remaining ingredients to the sugar and process until the mixture forms a ball. Turn out the mixture onto a lightly floured surface and knead a few times. Wrap the dough in plastic and refrigerate for 30 minutes (see Note).

Preheat the oven to 325°F. Line 2 cookie sheets with parchment paper or leave them ungreased.

Working with half of the dough at a time, roll the dough out until it is ¼-inch thick. Cut out desired shapes with cookie cutters. Place the cookies onto the baking sheets, leaving half an inch between each cookie. Repeat the rolling and cookie-cutting process until all of the dough has been used. It is all right to rework any scraps.

Note: The dough may be made in advance and refrigerated for up to 5 days before rolling out.

Bake the cookies for about 15 minutes or until they feel slightly firm when touched lightly. Remove from the oven and let them cool on the baking sheet for 5 minutes. They will be very fragile until the sugar hardens. Transfer to a wire rack to cool completely. Store the cookies in an airtight container for up to three days, or freeze in an airtight container for up to 4 weeks. Let the cookies come to room temperature before serving. I like to decorate them by drizzling melted chocolate or vanilla chips across the top.

Cream Cheese Cookies

Makes 36 cookies

If you believe, as I do, that there is no such thing as a pastry that is too rich or too flaky, this may prove to be your favorite recipe in the book. In fact, it was this recipe that got me the contract for the book! With one taste, pursed lips turn into smiles and disinterested glances turn into bright-eyed looks of excitement.

Although the dough is really a pastry, it is simple to make and easy to handle. The taste rewards will certainly outweigh the effort needed to roll out and shape the cookies.

1 cup (2 sticks) unsalted butter, at room temperature
¾ cup firm cream cheese, at room temperature
1½ cups unbleached all-purpose flour
1 cup apricot all-fruit spread

In a large bowl, roughly blend together the butter and cream cheese with a wooden spoon. Incorporate the flour, just until the dough is moist and clearly marbled with both the butter and cream cheese. Shape into a disk and wrap in plastic wrap. Refrigerate for 1 hour.

Preheat the oven to 375°F. Butter or line 2 cookie sheets with parchment paper.

To shape the cookies, work with one-quarter of the dough at a time, refrigerating the remaining dough until ready to use. On a lightly floured work surface, roll out the dough, working from the center and dusting the top and underside with flour as necessary, to form a square approximately 8 × 8 inches and that is a scant ¼-inch thick. Trim the edges to create a square. Cut into 9 equal squares by first dividing the whole piece vertically into thirds and then dividing the piece horizontally into thirds, like a tic-tac-toe board.

Place 1 scant teaspoon of jam into the center of each square. Lift all 4 corners of each square and bring them together over the jam. Pinch the corners until they hold together. It is not necessary to secure them with water because most of the cookies will open up during baking, which creates a pretty visual effect.

Place the cookies on the prepared baking sheets, leaving 1 inch of space around each. Refrigerate the shaped cookies while shaping the remaining dough. Chill the last batch for 10 minutes before baking. Bake for 20 to 25 minutes, or until the bottoms of the cookies are golden brown. Transfer to a wire rack to cool completely. Store in an airtight container for up to 4 days—if they last that long!

Date Squares

Makes 12 squares

I have always loved the naturally sweet taste of dates. So I've never under-stood the need to mask their flavor with sugar. This recipe lets the dates take center stage with only the addition of a little bit of citrus to balance out the sweetness.

Date filling

2 cups pitted unsweetened dates

½ cup water

2 teaspoons orange zest, finely chopped

2 tablespoons fresh orange juice

Crust and Topping

1 cup unbleached all-purpose flour

½ teaspoon baking soda

Pinch of salt

1 cup rolled oats

½ cup (1 stick) unsalted butter

¼ cup brown rice syrup

1 teaspoon pure vanilla extract

Preheat the oven to 350°F. Butter one 8 × 8-inch baking sheet.

To make the date filling: Combine the dates and the water in a medium nonreactive saucepan. Cook over medium heat, stirring to prevent the dates from sticking or burning. The dates will soften and form a paste as they absorb the water. Remove from the heat and stir in the orange zest and juice. Set aside.

To make the crust and topping: Sift together the flour, baking soda, and salt in a medium bowl. Add the rolled oats and stir to distribute.

In a small saucepan, melt the butter over medium heat. Remove from the heat and stir in the rice syrup and vanilla extract. Pour the butter mixture into the dry ingredients and stir until blended. Reserve one-third of the dough for the topping. Put the remaining two-thirds of the dough into the baking pan. Use your hands to pat the dough to cover the entire surface of the bottom of the pan. Prebake the crust for 5 minutes. Let cool.

Spread the date mixture evenly over the crust. Sprinkle the reserved dough over the dates. Bake for 20 to 25 minutes, or until the dough is very lightly browned. Let cool in the pan. Cut into 12 pieces.

Macaroons

Makes 12 cookies

In fewer than 20 minutes, you can have sweet mounds of chewy, shredded coconut baked until golden brown.

½ cup honey
2 large egg whites
1 teaspoon pure vanilla extract
Pinch of salt
3 cups unsweetened shredded coconut
½ cup semi-sweet grain-sweetened chocolate chips (see Note, page 101), chopped

Preheat the oven to 350°F. Line a baking sheet with parchment paper.

In a large bowl, mix together the honey, egg whites, vanilla extract, and salt. Stir in the coconut and chocolate chips. Wet your hands with cold water and gather the coconut mixture into approximately 2 heaping teaspoonful mounds. Place them onto the baking sheet about 1 inch apart. Bake for about 15 minutes or until the tops and bottoms are golden brown. Let the macaroons cool completely on the baking sheet before removing.

Note: The longer the mixture sits before shaping the runnier i gets, causing the macaroons to spread as they bake.

Double Chocolate Chip Cookies

Makes 24 cookies

If you really like chocolate, these are a must. The cocoa powder balances the sweetness of the maple sugar, and the result is a crisp, dark, rich cookie. You can drizzle melted vanilla-flavored chips over the tops, or put a chunk of your favorite naturally sweetened chocolate bar in the center of each cookie.

1 cup (2 sticks) unsalted butter, at room temperature

1½ cups maple sugar

2 large eggs

1 teaspoon pure vanilla extract

1½ cups unbleached all-purpose flour

1 cup unsweetened cocoa powder

1 teaspoon baking soda

½ teaspoon salt

2 cups semi-sweet grain-sweetened chocolate chips (see Note, page 101)

Preheat the oven to 325°F. Butter 2 cookie sheets or line each with parchment paper.

In the large bowl of an electric mixer, cream the butter and maple sugar, stopping to scrape down the sides of the bowl as necessary until light and fluffy. Add the eggs and vanilla. Continue to beat until the mixture is a light beige.

In a medium bowl, sift together the flour, cocoa, baking soda, and salt. Use a wooden spoon to stir the dry ingredients into the creamed mixture until blended. Mix in the chocolate chips.

Using heaping tablespoons of dough, form cookies into mounds. Place the mounds 2 inches apart on the prepared cookie sheets. Bake one sheet at a time in the middle of the oven for about 13 minutes, or until the centers have risen and the bottoms are set. Watch carefully—the dark color of the dough makes it difficult to determine when the cookies are done. Cool on the cookie sheet for 1 minute before using a large spatula to transfer them to a wire rack.

Mandel Bread

Makes 36 slices

In the late eighties, it was as though everyone discovered biscotti for the first time—even though Italians had been eating them for hundreds of years. The name derives from the method of "twice baking" the cookie (bi=2 times, cotto=cooked) to create a crisp accompaniment for a great café or for a glass of Vin Santo.

As the world was seeking out the perfect biscotti, I was fortunate enough not to have to go any further than my mother's kitchen. For years, she has made the best biscotti I've ever tried, only she calls them by their Jewish name, mandelbrot. One of my brother's friends in New York once said we should call them "biscotti Judaica." Whatever you call them, they are delicious. This recipe is an adaptation of my mother's recipe.

> **1 cup vegetable oil**
> **½ cup orange juice concentrate**
> **4 large eggs**
> **⅔ cup honey**
> **1 tablespoon pure vanilla extract**
> **4½ cups unbleached all-purpose flour**
> **2 teaspoons baking powder**
> **½ teaspoon salt**
> **2 cups whole raw almonds**

Preheat the oven to 350°F. Butter or line a baking sheet with parchment paper.

In a large bowl, mix together by hand or with an electric mixer the oil, orange juice concentrate, eggs, honey, and vanilla. Beat until well blended.

In a medium bowl, sift together the flour, baking powder, and salt. Using a wooden spoon, mix the dry ingredients into the liquid mixture until well incorporated.

Place the whole almonds into the bowl of a food processor fitted with the steel blade. Using the pulsing technique, coarsely chop the nuts to create a combination of both small and large pieces. Add the nuts to the batter, stirring just enough to incorporate. Do not overmix. The batter should be quite stiff.

To shape the cookies, divide the dough in half. Work on one side of the prepared baking sheet. Using your hands, form each portion of the dough into a log about 16 × 2 inches long, smoothing out the top and the sides as you go. Leave enough space between the logs to allow for the dough to expand.

Bake for 25 to 30 minutes. The dough will rise and the surface may crack. It is important for the logs to be baked through to the center, but not overbaked so they become too browned. The logs should be firm to the touch. Remove from the oven and let cool slightly.

Reduce the oven temperature to 225°F.

Using a sharp knife, cut the logs into ½-inch-thick slices. Lay the slices cut side down onto the baking sheet. Return the cookies to the oven and bake for 20 to 25 minutes, making sure the cookies are drying but not browning. Remove from the oven and turn the slices over. Return to the oven and continue baking for 20 to 25 more minutes until the second side is dry to the touch. Let the cookies cool completely. Store in an airtight container. The cookies will keep for up to 2 weeks.

Mincemeat Turnovers

Makes 36 cookies

For this dish, dried fruits are easily combined with sweet spices to make a naturally sweet mincemeat. I suggest you season the mixture to taste, and if you prefer no spice at all, squeeze a little lemon juice into the fruit to enhance the flavor. The filling and pastry will also work well as tarts.

Mincemeat filling

    8 ounces unsulphured pitted prunes

    4 ounces Thompson golden raisins, preferably organic

    ¼ cup chopped walnuts

    1 tablespoon lemon zest, finely chopped

    1 tablespoon dark rum

    1 teaspoon unsalted butter

    Ground cinnamon, ground cloves, and freshly grated nutmeg
       to taste

    Pinch of salt

Dough

    1 cup (2 sticks) unsalted butter, at room temperature

    2 cups unbleached all-purpose flour

    ½ cup sour cream

To prepare the filling: Combine the prunes and the raisins in a medium nonreactive saucepan. Pour in enough water to cover the fruit. Cook over medium heat, stirring with a wooden spoon, until the raisins are plump and the prunes are soft and begin to dissolve, about 10 minutes. Remove from the heat. Add the walnuts, lemon zest, rum, and butter. Season to taste with the spices and salt. (It makes about 1½ cups.)

    To prepare the dough: Combine the butter, flour, and sour cream in a large bowl. Working either with a wooden spoon or with your hands, mix the ingredients just until they form a dough. Wrap the dough in plastic wrap and refrigerate for at least 1 hour.

Note: The turnovers will keep unbaked in the freezer for up to 4 weeks. Before baking, defrost them for about 5 minutes. Brush with the egg wash just before baking and bake according to the above instructions.

Work with half of the dough at a time. On a lightly floured work surface, roll out the dough to a scant ⅛-inch thick. Cut into 3-inch squares. Place 1 teaspoon of filling toward the bottom right-hand corner of the square. Rub the perimeter of the square lightly with water.

To form a triangular turnover, fold the square diagonally in half, matching the top and bottom edges. Use the prongs of a fork to seal the edges of the dough together. Use a skewer to poke a steam hole in the top of the tart. Brush off any excess flour. Freeze the turn-overs for 5 minutes before baking. Brush with the egg wash and bake for about 12 minutes, or until the bottom of the pastry is golden brown.

Oatmeal Raisin Cookies

Makes 24 cookies

These are great, old-fashioned cookies. They are sweet and chewy with a hint of spice.

- ¾ cup (1½ sticks) unsalted butter, at room temperature
- 1½ cups maple sugar
- 2 large eggs
- 1 teaspoon pure vanilla extract
- 1½ cups unbleached all-purpose flour
- 1 teaspoon ground cinnamon
- 1 teaspoon baking soda
- ½ teaspoon salt
- 1 cup rolled oats
- 1 cup organic Thompson dark raisins

Preheat the oven to 325°F. Butter 2 cookie sheets or line each with parchment paper.

In the large bowl of an electric mixer, cream together the butter and the maple sugar, stopping to scrape down the sides of the bowl as necessary, until light and fluffy. Add eggs and vanilla and continue beating until the mixture is a light beige.

In a medium bowl, sift together the flour, cinnamon, baking soda, and salt. Toss the rolled oats into the sifted ingredients. Using a wooden spoon, stir the dry ingredients into the creamed mixture, just until both are blended. Mix in the raisins.

Form cookies into mounds using a heaping tablespoonful of dough. Place the mounds 2 inches apart on the prepared cookie sheets. Bake one sheet at a time in the middle of the oven for about 13 minutes, or until the centers have risen and the bottoms are golden brown. Cool on cookie sheet for 1 minute before using a large spatula to transfer them to a wire rack.

Orange Gingersnaps

Makes 36 cookies

These cookies are intensely flavored. Simple to prepare, they are great on their own or as a complement to either the Pear Cinnamon Ice Cream (page 146) or the Orange-Tarragon Sorbet (page 144).

¾ cup (1½ sticks) unsalted butter, at room temperature

2 cups maple sugar

2 tablespoons unsulfured molasses

2 large eggs

½ teaspoon pure vanilla extract

1 tablespoon orange zest, finely chopped

1½ tablespoons finely grated fresh ginger

3 cups unbleached all-purpose flour

1½ teaspoons baking soda

½ teaspoon salt

Preheat the oven to 375°F. Butter or line 2 large cookie sheets with parchment paper.

In the large bowl of an electric mixer, cream together the butter and maple sugar until light and fluffy, about 4 minutes. Add the molasses, eggs, and vanilla extract and continue beating for another 2 minutes. The mixture should end up light and fluffy. Mix in the orange zest and fresh ginger and beat until evenly distributed.

Into a medium bowl, sift together the flour, baking soda, and salt. Add the dry ingredients to the creamed butter mixture and stir with a wooden spoon until blended.

To shape the cookies, drop heaping teaspoonfuls onto the prepared cookie sheets, leaving 1½ inches of space between each to allow for spreading. As they bake, the cookies will rise and fall to form flat discs. Bake for about 10 minutes until the bottoms are lightly browned. Remove from the oven and let cool for a few minutes before transferring them to a wire rack to cool completely.

Peanut Butter Cookies

Makes 36 cookies

As we grow older, peanut butter and jelly sandwiches become taboo on the party circuit, but peanut butter cookies always remain in favor. They are neither pretentious nor unsophisticated. Try garnishing bite-sized cookies with a peanut in the center for something fancier. Either way they are sure to bring out the kid in all of us.

- ¾ cup (1½ sticks) unsalted butter
- 2 cups maple sugar
- 1¼ cups smooth natural peanut butter
- 2 large eggs
- 1 teaspoon pure vanilla extract
- 2½ cups unbleached all-purpose flour
- 1 teaspoon baking soda
- ½ teaspoon salt

Preheat the oven to 350°F. Butter 2 cookie sheets or line each with parchment paper.

In the large bowl of an electric mixer, cream together the butter, maple sugar, and peanut butter, stopping to scrape down the sides of the bowl as necessary, until light and fluffy. Add the eggs and vanilla and continue to beat until the mixture is pale yellow, about 2 minutes.

In a medium bowl, sift together the flour, baking soda, and salt. Using a wooden spoon, stir the dry ingredients into the creamed mixture. Stir just until both are blended.

Form the dough into balls using a heaping tablespoonful of dough for each cookie. Place the balls 2 inches apart on the prepared cookie sheets and flatten with the tines of a fork. Bake one sheet at a time in the middle of the oven for about 13 minutes, or until the centers have risen and the bottoms are lightly browned. Cool on the cookie sheet for 1 minute before using a large spatula to transfer them to a wire rack.

Making a Piping Tube

To make a piping tube, cut a piece of parchment paper about 12 × 12 inches long. Fold the paper on the diagonal. Cut along the fold. Use one half of the paper. With the cut side on the bottom, hold the paper between your left thumb and index finger. Starting at the bottom right hand corner of the paper, use your right hand to roll the paper toward yourself and into a cone shape. Adjust the size of the point by twisting the paper. A small point may be cut after the cone shape is secure and filled. When you have the desired point size, fold the top edges over and down into the cone until the shape is stable. Fill the cone to within an inch and a half from the top. To close the top, press the top opening closed and roll over the edges until you reach the filling.

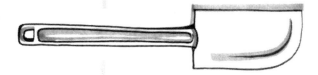

Peanut Butter Squares

Makes 20 squares

Kids of all ages will love the rich, smooth texture of the peanut butter mousse topping and the crunchy graham cracker crust. Drizzle melted chocolate over the top or serve with whipped cream (see box, page 68).

Crust

1 batch Graham Cracker Crust (page 219), omitting the cinnamon

Mousse

½ cup water

1 tablespoon unflavored gelatin

4 large eggs, separated, with whites at room temperature

½ cup honey

½ teaspoon salt

¾ cup unsweetened, unsalted peanut butter

⅓ cup water

1 teaspoon pure vanilla extract

Decoration

⅓ cup grain-sweetened chocolate chips (see Note, page 101)

½ teaspoon solid vegetable shortening

Preheat the oven to 350°F. Butter one 9 × 12-inch baking dish.

Press the crust into the prepared dish and bake until lightly browned, about 5 minutes. Let cool.

To prepare the mousse, place ½ cup of water in a small nonreactive saucepan and sprinkle the gelatin over top. Let soften for about 5 minutes.

In a small heat-proof bowl, beat the egg yolks until thick and lemon colored. Add the honey and salt, blending well. Place the gelatin over low heat and cook until dissolved. Stir into the yolk mixture. Place the bowl with the yolk mixture over simmering water and beat until thick and warm to the touch. Remove from the heat.

In a large bowl of an electric mixer, beat the peanut butter with ⅓ cup of water until blended. Stir the yolk mixture into the peanut butter. Add the vanilla extract. Chill until thick but not firm, about 15 minutes.

Using clean beaters and bowl, beat the egg whites with an electric mixer until stiff, but not dry. Stir one-quarter of the egg whites into the peanut butter mixture to lighten. Fold in the remaining egg whites. Gently pour the mixture over the crust. Cover with plastic wrap and chill until firm, about 4 hours or overnight. Cut into squares.

To decorate, melt the chocolate in a bowl set over simmering water, making sure the chocolate temperature doesn't exceed 120°F on a candy thermometer. If the chocolate is lumpy, add small amounts of the shortening until it reaches a drizzling consistency. Make a piping tube with a small hole out of parchment paper and fill with the warm chocolate. Drizzle thin lines diagonally across the surface of each square. The squares will keep refrigerated for 4 days.

Cookies and Squares

Rugelach

Makes 36 cookies

A traditional Jewish cookie often available in delicatessens, rugelach *are made with a rich cream cheese cookie dough that is rolled with raisins and nuts into crescents. Finished by a dip in cinnamon and sugar, they should be allowed to bake until the sugar begins to caramelize. Thanks to FruitSource and numerous trials, this recipe is sure to rival any other.*

Dough

1 batch Cream Cheese Cookies dough (page 103)

Filling

⅔ cup raspberry all-fruit spread

½ cup granular FruitSource (see Note, page 71)

1 tablespoon ground cinnamon

⅓ cup Thompson organic raisins

¼ cup walnuts, chopped

Egg glaze

1 large egg yolk

1 teaspoon water

Preheat the oven to 375°F. Butter or line a baking sheet with parchment paper.

Divide the dough into thirds and form each into a ball. Working with one ball at a time, on a lightly floured work surface, roll it out into a circle a scant ¼-inch thick. Cut the circle into 12 equal wedges. Without moving the wedges, spread some of the fruit spread over the dough.

In a small bowl, combine the FruitSource with the cinnamon and reserve half of the mixture for dipping. Sprinkle about 2 tablespoons of the cinnamon mixture over the layer of jam. Scatter one-third of the raisins and the nuts over the cinnamon mixture. Separate one wedge of dough. Starting at the base of the wedge, loosely roll the dough to form a crescent, ending with the point at the tip. Curl the ends toward the center.

In a small bowl, beat the egg yolk with the water to make the egg glaze. Brush the top and sides of each rugelach with the egg glaze. Dip them into the reserved cinnamon mixture, making sure to coat the entire glazed area. Place on the prepared baking sheet, cinnamon-dipped side up. Repeat with the remaining dough. If the dough starts to get soft, put the baking sheet into the refrigerator, chilling the crescents as you work.

Bake for about 25 minutes or until the rugelach are well browned. If the cookies are tightly rolled, make sure the centers are fully baked. Smaller crescents may be removed from the oven as they are done. Reduce the oven temperature to 325° to finish baking the centers of the larger rugelach. Let the cookies cool completely before serving.

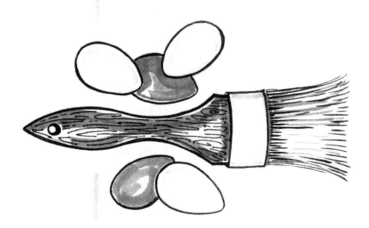

Sonny's Chocolate Walnut Brownies

Makes 9 squares

This is one of the easiest recipes to make. In fact, I whipped up a batch in the middle of catering a last-minute party for fifteen, when an hour before the guests were to arrive, the hostess was convinced there were not enough desserts. In addition to being able to mix the batter in the pot you melt the butter in, they only need to bake for 20 minutes. They were a big hit, as always, and nobody knew except me and the roasted potatoes that they were not part of the original plan!

½ **cup (1 stick) unsalted butter**
2½ **ounces unsweetened chocolate**
2 **extra-large eggs**
1 **cup maple sugar**
½ **teaspoon pure vanilla extract**
¾ **cup unbleached all-purpose flour**
Pinch of salt
½ **cup walnuts, chopped**

Preheat the oven to 350°F. Butter one 8 × 8-inch baking pan.

In a medium saucepan, melt the butter over medium heat. Once melted, remove from the heat and add the chocolate. Stir to melt the chocolate. Let cool slightly. The mixture should be just warm to the touch. If it is too hot, the eggs will form curds.

In a small bowl, beat the eggs with a fork until blended. While using a whisk to stir the warm chocolate mixture, pour in the eggs. Stir until thoroughly combined. Add the maple sugar and the vanilla and continue using the whisk to blend the ingredients.

Switch to a wooden spoon and stir the flour and salt into the chocolate mixture. Stir in the walnuts. Pour the batter into the prepared pan. Bake for about 25 minutes, or until the sides are firm and the center is still soft. To give the brownies a fudgey texture, it is important not to overbake them. Cool in the pan. Cut into squares.

Chapter Six

COOL AND CREAMY: ICE CREAMS, SORBETS, MOUSSES, AND MORE

*I*f you are looking for a selection of desserts that can be eaten with a spoon, this chapter is indispensable. Here are luscious mousses, silky ice creams, and refreshing sorbets. The ice cream bases can be sweetened with either honey or maple syrup.

Because mousses can be prepared in advance, they are perfect for entertaining. Many mass-produced ice creams are made with chemicals and air to prevent them from becoming hard as they sit for any extended periods of time in a freezer. Once you taste ice cream just out of your ice cream maker, you may never again have the problem of leftover ice cream. However, the amount of liquid sweeteners and liqueurs can help to minimize crystallization. In fact, my local maple syrup farmer told me he has yet to see maple syrup freeze. He suggests that it might freeze if you were working with it at the North Pole. In the unlikely event that you have ice cream left in the freezer long enough to become hard, it can be defrosted overnight in the refrigerator and put back in the ice-cream maker.

When preparing sorbets, use only the ripest and sweetest fruit. As with ice cream, the liquid sweeteners and liqueurs work to minimize crystallization. However, many sorbet recipes call for equal amounts of fruit purée to sugar syrup. The recipes in this chapter use sweeteners sparingly to allow for the fruit to be showcased. If they become hard, let the sorbet temper slightly before serving. The sorbets are also great for making frozen drinks. They can be combined with fruit juices and mixed in the blender. So hold the spoon and fill a glass instead!

Apricot Mascarpone Ice Cream

Makes about 1 quart; 8 servings

The slightly tart flavor of the apricots is balanced with the richness of the mascarpone cheese. Reserve a portion of the apricot purée to serve as a sauce.

16 ripe medium apricots
1 teaspoon freshly squeezed lemon juice
1 cup water
¾ cup maple syrup
¾ cup mascarpone cheese (see box, page 50)

Wash and pit the apricots. Place the apricots in the work bowl of a food processor fitted with the steel blade and purée until smooth. To remove any large pieces of skin, pass the purée through a strainer set over a bowl. There should be about 2½ cups of purée. Stir in the lemon juice.

In a medium saucepan, combine the water and maple syrup. Bring the liquid to a boil and let it reduce until you have 1½ cups remaining. Let cool. Stir the liquid into the fruit purée. Reserve 1 cup of the purée to serve as a sauce. In the food processor, combine the remaining purée with the mascarpone and process until smooth. Freeze in an ice-cream maker according to the manufacturer's instructions.

To serve, scoop the ice cream into individual bowls. Spoon the reserved apricot purée over each serving.

Apricot Sorbet

Makes about 1 quart; 8 servings

Apricots have a very subtle yet full-bodied flavor that creates a very distinctive sorbet. Choose ripe, sweet fruit that is not bruised. The flavor will intensify if the sorbet is allowed to "cure," or sit in the freezer for 2 to 4 hours before serving.

> **16 ripe medium apricots**
> **1 teaspoon freshly squeezed lemon juice**
> **1 cup water**
> **¾ cup maple syrup**

Wash and pit the apricots. Place the apricots in the bowl of a food processor fitted with the steel blade and purée until smooth. To remove any large pieces of skin, pass the purée through a strainer set over a bowl. There should be about 2½ cups of purée. Stir in the lemon juice.

In a medium saucepan, combine the water and maple syrup. Bring this to a boil and let the mixture reduce until 1½ cups remain. Cool. Stir the liquid into the fruit purée. Freeze in an ice-cream maker according to the manufacturer's instructions.

Arborio Rice Pudding

Makes about 4 cups; 4 servings

*Italian Arborio rice, a short-grain rice with a high starch content, is tradi-
tionally used for risotto. As hot liquid is added to the rice, the starch is
released, producing a creamy consistency. The technique requires you to
closely monitor the cooking, but the procedure is not complicated. The pudding is best served chilled.*

½ cup Arborio rice

3 cups whole milk

2 large egg yolks

⅓ cup maple syrup

½ cup heavy cream

¼ teaspoon salt

½ teaspoon pure vanilla extract

½ teaspoon ground cinnamon

¼ teaspoon freshly ground nutmeg

½ cup organic Thompson dark raisins

In a large saucepan, bring about 2 cups of water to a boil. Add the rice
and cook for 1 minute. Immediately drain the rice, discarding the
cooking water. Pour the milk into the saucepan and add the rice. Cook
over medium-low heat, stirring often to prevent the rice from sticking and to prevent a skin from forming on the surface. Continue
cooking until the rice is soft to the bite, but retains its shape and the
milk has been absorbed, about 45 minutes. Remove from the heat.

In a small bowl, mix the egg yolks with the maple syrup. To
prevent the yolks from curdling, temper the yolks by stirring in a
spoonful of the hot rice mixture. Stirring the rice constantly, pour
in the yolk mixture. Return to the heat and continue stirring while
the mixture cooks for another few minutes.

Add the cream and cook until the mixture is steaming, about 2
mintues. Remove from the heat and add the salt, vanilla extract, cinnamon, nutmeg, and raisins. Pour into a bowl. Cover with plastic
wrap pressed to the surface and chill until ready to serve.

Banana Kahlúa Ice Cream

Makes about 1 quart; 6 servings

Bananas are so flavorful they can be prepared in many ways. Although you can freeze bananas without cream and blend them to make a delicious and satisfying frozen dessert, here I have included and teamed the bananas with a hint of Kahlúa for a sophisticated ice cream.

5 very ripe bananas

¼ cup Kahlúa, or other coffee-flavored liqueur

2 cups whole milk

5 large egg yolks

⅓ cup maple syrup

1 cup heavy cream

1 teaspoon pure vanilla extract

In a nonstick frying pan, mash the bananas and mix with 2 tablespoons of the Kahlúa. Cook over low heat until the bananas dissolve, about 35 minutes. Purée in a food processor or blender and let cool.

In a separate medium saucepan, bring the milk to a simmer over medium-high heat. Meanwhile, in a large bowl, beat the egg yolks with the maple syrup until the mixture becomes thick and pale yellow, either by hand or with an electric mixer.

While stirring the egg yolks with a whisk, gradually add half of the milk. Once blended, add the remaining milk. Pour the mixture into a clean saucepan and cook over medium heat, stirring constantly with a wooden spoon, until the mixture thickens enough to coat the spoon. Remove from the heat and add the heavy cream.

Pour the mixture through a strainer set over a large bowl. Add the remaining Kahlúa and the vanilla extract. Refrigerate until chilled, about 2 hours. Stir in the banana purée. Freeze in an ice-cream maker according to the manufacturer's instructions.

Basmati Rice Pudding

Makes about 3½ cups; 4 servings

This is a classic comfort food.

½ cup basmati rice
2½ cups whole milk
Seeds from 1 green cardamom pod
¼ teaspoon freshly ground nutmeg
1 large egg yolk
¼ cup maple syrup
½ cup heavy cream
¼ teaspoon salt
½ teaspoon pure vanilla extract
½ cup organic Thompson dark raisins
1 tablespoon unsalted butter
½ cup blanched almonds, coarsely chopped

In a large saucepan, bring about 2 cups of water to a boil. Add the rice and cook for 1 minute. Immediately drain the rice, discarding the cooking water. Pour the milk into the saucepan and add the rice. Put the seeds from the cardamom pod into the milk; add the nutmeg.

Cook over medium-low heat, stirring often to prevent the rice from sticking and a skin from forming on the surface. Continue cooking until the rice is soft to the bite, but retains its shape and the milk has been absorbed, about 45 minutes. Remove from the heat.

In a small bowl, mix the egg yolk with the maple syrup. To temper the yolk, stir in a spoonful of the rice mixture. Stirring the rice constantly, pour in the yolk mixture. Return to the heat and continue stirring for another few minutes. Add the cream and cook until the mixture is steaming. Remove from the heat and add the salt, vanilla extract, and raisins. Pour into a bowl. Cover with plastic wrap pressed to the surface and chill until ready to serve.

Melt the butter in a frying pan. Add the almonds and cook over medium heat until golden brown, about 3 minutes. Serve the pudding sprinkled with the nuts.

Black Raspberry Ripple Ice Cream

Makes about 1 quart; 6 servings

Ripples come in many flavors. Here, ice cream flavored with blackberry liqueur is rippled with a black raspberry sauce.

Ice cream

- 2 cups whole milk
- 5 large egg yolks
- ½ cup maple syrup
- 1 cup heavy cream
- ½ cup blackberry-flavored liqueur

Ripple sauce

- ½ cup maple syrup
- 1½ cups black raspberries, red raspberries, or blackberries
- 2 tablespoons blackberry flavored liqueur
- ⅛ teaspoon ground cinnamon
- Lemon juice to taste (1 to 2 teaspoons)

In a medium saucepan, bring the milk to a simmer. Meanwhile, in a large bowl, beat the egg yolks with the maple syrup until thick and pale yellow, either by hand or with an electric mixer.

While stirring the egg yolks with a whisk, gradually add half of the milk. Once blended, add the remaining milk. Pour the mixture into a clean large saucepan and cook over medium heat, stirring constantly with a wooden spoon, until the mixture thickens enough to coat the spoon. Remove from the heat and add the cream. Pour the mixture through a strainer set over a large bowl. Refrigerate until chilled, about 2 hours.

While the ice cream base is chilling, prepare the ripple sauce. In a heavy saucepan, bring the maple syrup to a boil. Add the berries and cook until tender, about 5 minutes. Remove berry pieces with a slotted spoon and reserve. Add the liqueur, cinnamon, and lemon juice to taste to the maple syrup mixture and boil the liquid until it is reduced by half. Combine it with the reserved berries and allow to cool.

To make the finished ice cream, just before freezing add the liqueur. Freeze in an ice-cream maker according to the manufacturer's instructions. Transfer the ice cream to a storage container, layering it with spoonfuls of the ripple sauce, ending with a layer of ice cream.

Blood Orange Sorbet

Makes about 1 quart; 8 servings

Blood oranges are another great food I discovered in Italy. The first time I was there it was mid-March. Every espresso bar had a large pitcher of a dark pink juice on the counter, and for a few thousand lire you could drink the sweet nectar of this most unusual fruit. Ginger is a nice complement to the complex flavor. Try serving the sorbet with Orange Gingersnaps (page 113).

3½ cups fresh blood-orange juice
½ cup honey

In a large bowl, combine the juice and the honey. Freeze in an ice-cream maker according to the manufacturer's instructions. To enhance the flavor, transfer the sorbet to an airtight container and freeze for at least 2 hours before serving.

Butternut Squash Custard

Makes six ⅔-cup ramekins

I have limited the amount of spices to avoid masking the light flavor of the butternut squash.

- **1 medium butternut squash, about 2 pounds**
- **3 large eggs**
- **1 cup half-and-half**
- **⅓ cup brown rice syrup**
- **¼ cup date sugar**
- **1½ teaspoons ground cinnamon**
- **½ teaspoon freshly ground nutmeg**
- **Pinch of freshly ground black pepper**
- **½ teaspoon of salt**

Preheat the oven to 400°F. Bake the squash until tender, about 45 minutes. Remove from the oven and let cool. Peel and remove the seeds of the squash and purée the flesh in a blender or food processor. You should have about 2 cups. Reduce the oven temperature to 350°F.

Butter six ⅔-cup ramekins. Have ready a baking dish large enough to create a bain-marie (see box, page 24).

In a large bowl, mix together the squash purée, eggs, half-and-half, brown rice syrup, date sugar, and all the spices. Fill each ramekin with the squash mixture. Set the ramekins in the baking dish and pour hot water into the dish to reach half-way up the sides of the ramekins. Bake for about 20 minutes or until the centers have risen and the filling has set.

Serve chilled or warm. Garnish with a dollop of whipped cream or *crème fraîche* (see box, page 163).

Caramel Custard

Makes about 3½ cups; 6 servings

It has been suggested that combining custard with caramelized sugar was developed during the early nineteenth century when sugar was less expensive and more accessible due to mass production. However, once you taste this combination made with maple syrup, you may wonder whether maple syrup was used instead of sugar before the industrial age.

1 cup maple syrup
2 tablespoons water
2½ cups whole milk
3 large eggs
3 large egg yolks
½ cup maple syrup or honey
1 teaspoon pure vanilla extract
Pinch of salt
2 tablespoons flavored liqueur, such as Kahlúa or Grand Marnier

Preheat the oven to 350°F. Have ready six ⅔-cup ramekins and a pan large enough to hold the ramekins in a water bath to sit in and be surrounded by water to create a bain-marie (see box, page 24).

In a medium nonreactive heavy saucepan, combine the maple syrup and water. Caramelize according to the instructions on page 132. Coat the bottom and sides of the ramekins with the caramel.

In a medium saucepan, warm the milk over medium heat.

In a mixing bowl, stir the eggs, yolks, and sweetener, without creating foam, until blended. Stir in the warm milk. Add the vanilla extract and salt. Pass the mixture through a strainer set over a bowl. Using a ladle, distribute the custard evenly among the ramekins.

Set the ramekins in a baking dish and pour in boiling water to surround them about half-way up the sides. Bake for 20 to 25 minutes, or until the custard is just set and a skewer inserted ⅛-inch deep along the side comes out clean. Let cool at least 10 minutes before serving.

Whether you are serving the custard chilled or warm, do not loosen the edges until just prior to presenting. To unmold, run a knife along the edge to loosen the custard and cover with the serving plate. Invert the plate, allowing the caramel to run over the custard. Spoon 1 teaspoon of flavored liqueur over each custard. Serve immediately.

Carmelizing Maple Syrup

Caramelizing maple syrup uses the same principles as caramelizing refined sugar; however, since the color of the maple syrup is brown, it requires you to rely heavily on your sense of smell. In a heavy saucepan, combine the maple syrup and the water and bring to a boil over medium heat. As the mixture boils, occasionally swirl the pan to stir the syrup. Continue boiling until the syrup begins to smell faintly burnt. This aroma lets you know the mixture is beginning to caramelize. Once it reaches this stage, the syrup will cook more rapidly, and you must work quickly. Unlike caramelizing refined sugar, when maple syrup begins to caramelize, the sugar becomes its own heat conductor. Maple syrup requires you to put the saucepan on and off the heat until the desired degree of caramelizing has been reached.

Chocolate Bourbon Ice Cream

Makes about 1 quart; 6 servings

Even before this ice cream base is frozen, it is so thick you can only imagine how decadent the flavor will be. For even more flavor and texture, let your imagination run wild and add pieces of your favorite Tropical Source chocolate bar (see Note, page 99).

2 cups whole milk

5 large egg yolks

½ cup maple syrup

1 cup heavy cream

1 cup semi-sweet grain-sweetened chocolate chips (see Note, page 101), melted

¼ cup bourbon

In a medium saucepan, bring the milk to a simmer. Meanwhile, in a bowl, beat the egg yolks with the maple syrup until thick and pale yellow, either by hand or with an electric mixer, about 4 minutes.

While stirring the egg yolks with a whisk, gradually add half of the milk. Once blended, add the remaining milk. Pour the mixture into a clean large saucepan and cook over medium heat, stirring constantly with a wooden spoon, until the mixture thickens enough to coat the spoon. Remove from the heat and add the cream.

Pour the mixture through a strainer set over a clean bowl. Stir in the melted chocolate chips. Refrigerate mixture until chilled. Just before freezing, add the bourbon. Freeze in an ice-cream maker according to the manufacturer's instructions.

Cool and Creamy: Ice Creams, Sorbets, Mousses, and More

Honey Mousse with Spiced Plum Sauce

Makes one 3-cup mold; 8 servings

The sweet honey flavor of the mousse is complemented by the tart, lightly spiced fresh plum sauce. Serve the leftover sauce with pancakes.

Mousse

- 1 tablespoon unflavored gelatin
- ¼ cup water
- 3 large egg yolks
- ½ cup honey
- 1 teaspoon pure vanilla extract
- 1 cup heavy cream
- 3 egg whites, at room temperature

Sauce

- 3 pounds black plums
- 3 whole cloves
- ½ teaspoon ground cinnamon
- 2 to 4 tablespoons honey
- 1 teaspoon orange zest, chopped

Have ready a decorative 6-cup bowl.

In a small saucepan, sprinkle the gelatin over the water. Let soften for 5 minutes.

Meanwhile, in the large bowl of an electric mixer, beat together the egg yolks, honey, and vanilla extract until thick and light. Cook the gelatin over very low heat until dissolved, and beat into the honey mixture. Chill until slightly thickened, about 10 minutes. Watch carefully because the mixture will firm up quickly. If the honey separates, beat until blended.

In a chilled bowl, beat the heavy cream until stiff. Mix ¼ of the whipped cream into the honey mixture to loosen. Fold in the remaining whipped cream. Using clean beaters, beat the egg whites until stiff but not dry. Fold into the honey mixture. Gently transfer to the decorative bowl. Cover with plastic wrap and chill for 3 hours or until set. This may be prepared the day before.

To prepare the sauce, cut the plums into quarters, removing the stones, and place in a nonreactive saucepan. Add the cloves. Cook over low heat, stirring occasionally. It will take a few minutes for the juice to start coming out of the plums. As more juice comes out, add the cinnamon. Continue cooking until the fruit breaks down, about 20 minutes. Depending on the natural sweetness of the plums, add honey to taste. Add the orange zest. Remove the cloves. Transfer the mixture to a blender or food processor fitted with a steel blade and blend until smooth. (Makes about 2 cups.) Chill until ready to serve. Serve on the side with the mousse.

Lemon Strawberry Ice Cream

Makes about 1 quart; 6 servings

If you do not have any strawberries, the lemon custard makes a great ice cream on its own. But the combination is even better.

¼ cup plus 1 tablespoon fresh lemon juice
½ cup honey
Zest of 2 lemons, finely chopped
1 cup half-and-half
2 large egg yolks
Pinch of salt
1 cup heavy cream
1½ cup sliced strawberries
2 tablespoons honey

In a small bowl, combine the lemon juice, honey, and lemon zest. Let stand for 30 minutes.

In a small nonreactive saucepan, scald the half-and-half, heating it over medium heat and set aside.

In a large bowl of an electric mixer, beat the egg yolks with the salt until well blended. Gradually pour in the warm scalded half-and-half. Transfer the mixture to a clean saucepan and cook over medium heat, stirring constantly with a wooden spoon, until the mixture thickens enough to coat the spoon. Remove from the heat and pass the custard through a strainer set over a clean bowl. Stir in the lemon juice mixture and the heavy cream. Cover with plastic wrap pressed to the surface and chill.

Meanwhile, in a medium nonreactive bowl, toss the strawberries with the honey and lemon juice; let stand until the custard is chilled. Begin freezing the lemon custard in an ice cream maker according to the manufacturer's instructions. Halfway before the custard is completely frozen, add the strawberries and any juice. Continue freezing according to the manufacture's instructions.

Strawberry Banana Yogurt Smoothy

Makes about one 10-ounce glass; 1 serving

Slowly sipping a cool, creamy fruit drink can be a great way to finish dinner on a hot summer night. If you don't have any Strawberry Sorbet, substitute frozen fresh berries or chunks of banana. A little rum doesn't hurt either.

½ cup Strawberry Sorbet (see below)
1 ripe medium banana
¼ cup apple juice
½ cup plain low-fat yogurt

In a blender or the work bowl of a food processor fitted with the steel blade, combine all the ingredients. Blend until smooth. Pour into a chilled glass and serve immediately.

Strawberry Sorbet

Makes about 1 quart; 8 servings

Strawberries mark the start of the local berry season, and you will want to wait until that time before you attempt to make this recipe. You won't be able to match the bright red color or the luscious flavor of these in-season fruits.

6 cups local strawberries, hulled and sliced
½ cup maple syrup
2 tablespoons honey
2 teaspoons fresh lemon juice

In a large nonreactive bowl, combine all the ingredients and let sit for 30 minutes. Transfer to a blender or a food processor fitted with the steel blade, and purée until smooth. Freeze in an ice-cream maker according to the manufacturer's instructions.

Cool and Creamy: Ice Creams, Sorbets, Mousses, and More

Lychee Ice Cream

Makes about 1 quart; 6 servings

The first time I had lychee-flavored ice cream was on a warm summer night after a Chinese dinner in New York City's Chinatown. If you aren't familiar with them, lychees will be an amazing flavor discovery. Peeling away the rough skin exposes the succulent, translucent flesh, which is then easily loosened from the smooth interior stone. The lychee's flavor is intoxicating.

1¾ cups milk

4 large eggs

⅓ cup maple syrup

¾ cup heavy cream

1 teaspoon pure vanilla extract

1½ pounds fresh lychee fruit

1 tablespoon honey (optional)

In a medium saucepan, bring the milk to a simmer. Meanwhile, in a bowl, beat the egg yolks with the maple syrup until thick and pale yellow, either by hand or with an electric mixer.

While stirring the egg yolks with a whisk, gradually add half of the milk. Once blended, add the remaining milk. Pour the mixture into a clean large saucepan and cook over medium heat, stirring constantly with a wooden spoon, until the mixture thickens enough to coat the spoon. Remove from the heat and add the heavy cream.

Pour the mixture through a strainer set over a large bowl. Stir in the vanilla extract. Refrigerate the mixture until chilled, about 2 hours.

Just before freezing, peel the lychees over a bowl to catch any juice, and separate the flesh from the stone. Do not worry if the inside of the flesh is slightly brown from the stone. In a blender or food processor, chop the fruit and juice into small chunks; do not purée. You should have about 1½ cups of fruit and juice. Taste, and if it is slightly sour, mix in the honey. Stir the fruit mixture into the custard. Freeze in an ice cream maker according to the manufacturer's instructions.

Malt Ice Cream

Makes about 1 quart; 6 servings

Although this recipe was specifically developed for the Banana Chocolate Crêpes (page 188), that doesn't mean you can't enjoy it on its own!

2 cups whole milk
5 large egg yolks
½ cup maple syrup
1 tablespoon barley malt syrup
1 cup heavy cream

In a medium saucepan, bring the milk to a simmer. Meanwhile, in a bowl, beat the egg yolks with the maple and barley malt syrups until thick and pale yellow, either by hand or with an electric mixer.

While stirring the egg yolks with a whisk, gradually add half of the milk. Once blended, add the remaining milk. Pour the mixture into a clean, large saucepan and cook over medium heat, stirring constantly with a wooden spoon, until the mixture thickens enough to coat the spoon. Remove from the heat and add the cream.

Pour the mixture through a strainer set over a large bowl. Refrigerate the mixture until chilled, about 2 hours. Freeze in an ice cream maker according to the manufacturer's instructions.

Mango Gelato

Makes about 1 quart; 6 servings

I was on my way to get the Sunday New York Times *when I passed a fruit stand filled with sweet ripe mangoes. How could I resist? Look for soft, ripe mangoes oozing with sweet sap.*

1¾ cups milk

4 large eggs

⅓ cup maple syrup

¾ cup heavy cream

1 teaspoon pure vanilla extract

2 large very ripe mangoes

2 teaspoons freshly squeezed lemon juice

In a medium saucepan, bring the milk to a simmer. Meanwhile, in a large bowl, beat the egg yolks with the maple syrup until thick and pale yellow, either by hand or with an electric mixer.

While stirring the egg yolks with a whisk, gradually add half of the milk. Once blended, add the remaining milk. Pour the mixture into a clean large saucepan and cook over medium heat, stirring constantly with a wooden spoon, until the mixture thickens enough to coat the spoon. Remove from the heat and add the heavy cream.

Pour the mixture through a strainer set over a large bowl. Stir in the vanilla extract. Refrigerate the mixture until chilled, about 2 hours.

Just before freezing, peel the mangoes and remove the flesh from the pit without removing the stringy fibers. Purée in a blender or food processor until smooth. Add the lemon juice. You should have about 1½ cups of purée. Stir the mango into the custard. Freeze in an ice cream maker according to manufacturer's instructions.

Mango Yogurt Mousse

Makes 6 servings

The mangoes create a luscious, exotic taste. Look for ripe mangoes that are oozing clear, sweet sap and have a sweet aroma. The rich, creamy texture of the mousse is enhanced with the smallest amount of gelatin; it sets without becoming too firm. Serve it in ramekins garnished with raspberry coulis and whipped cream (see box, page 68).

2 large very ripe mangoes
3 tablespoons cold water
1 tablespoon plain gelatin
1½ cups plain yogurt
2 to 3 tablespoons honey
1 cup heavy cream

Peel the mangoes and remove the flesh from the pit without removing the stringy fibers. Purée in a blender or food processor until smooth. You should have about 1½ cups. Pour the fruit into a mixing bowl.

In a small saucepan, pour the cold water and sprinkle in the gelatin. Let sit for 5 minutes. Cook over medium heat until the gelatin is dissolved, but do not boil. Pour the dissolved gelatin into the puréed mango and mix thoroughly. Stir in the yogurt and add the honey to taste. The mixture should be slightly tart, depending on the natural sweetness of the mangoes being used.

In a chilled, large bowl, whip the heavy cream until stiff (see box, page 68). Stir in one-third of the whipped cream to lighten the mango mixture. Fold in the remaining whipped cream. Pour the mousse into serving dishes. Cover with plastic wrap and refrigerate for at least 3 hours. Serve with berry *coulis* and more whipped cream.

Maple Syrup Mousse

Makes 8 servings

Since Canada supplies the world with 70 percent of its maple syrup, it seems only fitting to showcase this distinct flavor with another of Canada's great culinary treasures—this recipe's creator, my friend, Bonnie Stern. Bonnie has been a Canadian ambassador of fine food since she opened her cooking school in 1973. The Bonnie Stern School of Cooking has become Toronto's place to meet and learn from the world's greatest chefs. I was more than delighted when, without hesitation, Bonnie agreed to let me include her recipe.

¼ cup cold water
1 tablespoon unflavored gelatin
1 cup maple syrup
3 large egg yolks
1 teaspoon pure vanilla extract
2 tablespoons coffee liqueur
2½ cups heavy cream

Have ready 8 dessert glasses.

In a small saucepan, pour the cold water and sprinkle in the gelatin. Let soften for 5 minutes. In a separate saucepan, bring the maple syrup to a boil. Heat the gelatin mixture just until it dissolves, about 30 seconds.

In a large heat-proof bowl, beat the egg yolks and slowly whisk in the hot maple syrup. Whisk in the gelatin mixture. Place the bowl over simmering water and heat the egg yolk mixture until it becomes slightly custardy, about 5 minutes. Remove from the heat and stir in the vanilla extract and liqueur. Cool to room temperature either by placing the bowl over ice or in the refrigerator. Do not allow the gelatin to set. (If it does set, place the bowl in a larger bowl of hot water until the mixture becomes liquid.)

In a chilled large bowl, whip the heavy cream until soft peaks form. Fold it gently into the maple base. Spoon the mousse into the dessert glasses and chill for at least 1 hour before serving.

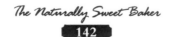

Grand Marnier–Caramel Gelato

Makes about 1 quart; 6 servings

The sweet taste of caramel is combined with the refreshing flavor of orange for a rich, satisfying cool dessert. Try serving it with Orange Gingersnaps (page 113).

¾ cup maple syrup

1 cup heavy cream

2 cups whole milk

5 large egg yolks

3 tablespoons Grand Marnier, or other orange-flavored liqueur

Into a heavy medium saucepan, pour half of the maple syrup and cook over medium-high heat until it bubbles and begins to caramelize (see box, page 132). Remove from the heat and carefully add the heavy cream to stop the cooking process. Stir the cream mixture until all the caramel has dissolved and set aside.

In a separate medium saucepan, bring the milk to a simmer. Meanwhile, in a bowl, beat the egg yolks with the remaining maple syrup until thick and pale yellow, either by hand or with an electric mixer.

While stirring the egg yolks with a whisk, gradually add half of the milk. Once blended, add the remaining milk. Pour the mixture into a clean large saucepan and cook over medium heat, stirring constantly with a wooden spoon, until the mixture thickens enough to coat the spoon. Remove from the heat and add the cream mixture.

Pour the mixture through a strainer set over a clean bowl. Add the orange liqueur. Refrigerate until chilled, about 2 hours. Freeze in an ice cream maker according to the manufacturer's instructions.

Orange-Tarragon Sorbet

Makes about 1 quart; 8 servings

The licorice flavor of the tarragon is balanced by the sweet flavor of the orange juice.

3½ cups fresh orange juice
½ cup honey
1 heaping tablespoon fresh tarragon, finely chopped

In a large bowl, combine the orange juice and the honey, stirring until dissolved. Add the tarragon. Freeze in an ice-cream maker according to manufacturer's instructions. To enhance the flavor, freeze the sorbet for about 4 hours before serving.

Ouzo Ice Cream

Makes about 1 quart; 6 servings

Combining rich, creamy custard with the cool anise flavor of Ouzo creates a very sophisticated and refreshing adult ice cream.

2 cups whole milk
5 large egg yolks
½ cup honey
1 cup heavy cream
½ cup Ouzo, or other anise-flavored liqueur

In a medium saucepan, bring the milk to a simmer. Meanwhile, in a separate saucepan, beat the egg yolks with the honey until thick and pale yellow, either by hand or with an electric mixer.

While stirring the egg yolks with a whisk, gradually add half of the milk. Once blended, add the remaining milk. Pour the mixture into a clean large saucepan and cook over medium heat, stirring constantly with a wooden spoon, until the mixture thickens enough to coat the spoon. Remove from the heat and add the cream.

Pour the mixture through a strainer set over a large bowl. Refrigerate the mixture until chilled, about 2 hours. Just before freezing, add the Ouzo. Freeze in an ice cream maker according to the manufacturer's instructions.

Pineapple-Ginger Sorbet

Makes about 1 quart; 8 servings

I usually go to the market with an idea of what I am looking for, but I have learned over the years never to be afraid to completely abandon the first idea when a great culinary opportunity presents itself. One day, I was looking for ripe pears when I saw the perfect pineapple. If you are not in possession of the perfect pineapple, proceed at your own risk!

½ cup honey

1 cup water

One 1-inch piece fresh ginger

1 very ripe fresh pineapple, to make 3 cups purée

In a small saucepan, combine the honey and water. Slice the ginger into about 6 thin pieces. Add to the liquid mixture and cook over medium-high heat. Bring the mixture to a boil and reduce by about one-third, leaving 1 cup. Let the ginger steep as it cools. Pass the ginger mixture through a strainer.

Peel and core the pineapple, making sure to remove any hard, fibrous parts of the rind. Cut into chunks and purée in a food processor or blender. Transfer the purée to a large bowl and add the honey-ginger syrup. Freeze in an ice-cream maker according to the manufacturer's instructions.

Pear Cinnamon Ice Cream

Makes about 1 quart; 6 servings

The first time I had pear ice cream was during a vacation in Paris. After walking through the city, my brother and I stopped to get some ice cream. We decided to share a cone. I remember they had cones specifically for two flavors; unlike in North America where we just pile the second flavor on top of the first, the Parisian cone had a place for the second scoop so the two flavors would be side by side, or à côté.

Although the delicious flavor is still memorable, I could never forget what happened next. After we got our ice cream, we went to pay not realizing we had spent almost all of our money. We managed to scrape together 50 francs leaving us about 2 francs short, which at the time was equal to 20 cents. The clerk was not impressed. Fortunately, my brother had spent the previous six months living in France and was able to explain the situation as if he were a local, with all the appropriate gestures and intonations.

The pear purée combines with the custard to create a lighter ice cream balanced by the warmth of the spicy cinnamon.

1¾ cups milk

4 large egg yolks

⅓ cup maple syrup

¾ cup heavy cream

1 teaspoon pure vanilla extract

6 very ripe pears

1 teaspoon fresh lemon juice

3 tablespoons honey

¾ teaspoon ground cinnamon

In a medium saucepan, bring the milk to a simmer. Meanwhile, in a bowl, beat the egg yolks with the maple syrup until thick and pale yellow, either by hand or with an electric mixer.

While stirring the egg yolks with a whisk, gradually add half of the milk. Once blended, add the remaining milk. Pour the mixture into a clean, large saucepan and cook over medium heat, stirring constantly with a wooden spoon, until the mixture thickens enough to coat the spoon. Remove from the heat and add the heavy cream.

Pour the mixture through a strainer set over a large bowl. Stir in the vanilla extract. Refrigerate the mixture until chilled, about 2 hours.

Just before freezing, peel the pears and slice into chunks. In a large nonreactive bowl, toss with the lemon juice, the honey, and the cinnamon. Purée in a blender or food processor until smooth. You should have about 2 cups of purée. Stir the pear mixture into the custard. Freeze in an ice-cream maker according to manufacturer's instructions.

Cool and Creamy: Ice Creams, Sorbets, Mousses, and More

Raspberry Mousse

Makes 8 servings

Surprisingly, frozen raspberries work really well for this mousse. Find organically grown berries in the freezer section of your health food store.

2 cups unsweetened frozen raspberries (10-ounce package), thawed

1 tablespoon fresh lemon juice

6 tablespoons water

1 tablespoon unflavored gelatin

2 large egg yolks

½ cup plus 2 tablespoons maple syrup

1 tablespoon orange flavored liqueur

2 cups heavy cream

½ pint fresh raspberries

Have ready 8 large wine glasses.

In the work bowl of a food processor fitted with the steel blade, combine the frozen raspberries and any juice with the lemon juice. Pulse the machine on and off a few times to break up the berries, leaving some large pieces; do not purée. Transfer to a bowl.

In a small saucepan, pour the cold water and sprinkle in the gelatin. Let soften for 5 minutes. Cook over low heat to dissolve. Stir the dissolved gelatin into the raspberry mixture, blending thoroughly.

In a large bowl, beat the egg yolks and ½ cup maple syrup together until thick and lemon colored. Beat in the liqueur. Set the bowl over simmering water. Stirring constantly with a whisk, heat until thickened and hot to the touch.

Let cool to room temperature. Stir in the raspberry mixture and chill until just beginning to set, about 20 minutes.

In a chilled, large bowl, whip the heavy cream with the 2 tablespoons of maple syrup until stiff. Working quickly, fold the cream into the berry mixture until it is completely blended. Spoon into the wine glasses and let set in the refrigerator for at least 4 hours. The mousse will keep for 2 days. Serve garnished with fresh berries.

Chapter Seven

PASTRY: PIES, TARTS, STRUDELS, AND MORE

*F*or me, pastry could be classified as one of the natural wonders of the world. How does the combination of a few simple ingredients— flour, butter, and water—come together to create such a rich, mouth-watering, delectable foundation for both sweet and savory delights? Granted, there is a world of heavy, tough, and soggy baked goods that masquerade as pastry, but with one bite of the real stuff, I am reminded that anything is possible.

Too often, pastry-making can become a stressful experience. It may take a few attempts to master the technique for the classic pastry recipe I recommend, but it will be worth the practice. I hope these attempts remain fun, because even though I think pastry is truly amazing, it remains "only pastry." Some helpful hints are to blind bake the crust and, to ensure for a crisp bottom crust, bake it on the oven's bottom rack.

For variety, this chapter contains other sorts of flaky treats, such as strudels prepared with frozen phyllo sheets and tarts made with sweet crusts, which are the most forgiving. All these can be made small or large and filled with creams or fruits, or both. Let your imagination run wild.

Apple Custard Tart

Makes one 10-inch tart; 8 servings

For this classic dessert, brown rice syrup is a perfect alternative to white sugar; it makes the custard creamy. Cooked fruit and custard are one of my favorite combinations. Although the custard has a tendency to shrink from around the apples, you can garnish the top with nuts or honey.

1 batch Sweet Tart Pastry (page 233)
2 large baking apples, peeled and cored (see box, page 153)
2 tablespoons brown rice syrup
2 large eggs
1 cup heavy cream
1 teaspoon pure vanilla extract

Note: If the custard shrinkage concerns you, decorate by toasting some sliced almonds and sprinkling them over the top of the tart, brush the top with warmed honey.

Preheat the oven to 350°F.

Prepare the pastry according to the directions on page 157 to make one 10-inch tart shell. Bake for about 15 minutes or until the center is lightly browned. Let cool.

Slice the apples into ¼-inch-thick wedges and position on the tart shell to form concentric circles. In a medium bowl, combine the brown rice syrup, eggs, cream, and vanilla extract. Beat with a whisk until all the ingredients are well blended making sure the brown rice syrup is thoroughly dissolved. Pour the cream mixture over the apples. Bake for about 20 minutes or until the custard has set. Remove from the oven and let cool. Serve warm or at room temperature.

Pastry: Pies, Tarts, Strudels, and More

Apple Pie

Makes one 8-inch, deep-dish pie; 8 servings

In the town of Kleinburg, Ontario, the first Saturday after Labor Day is their annual Binder Twine Festival. Although the festival dates back to the 1890s when Charles Shaw, Jr. began distributing twine to local farmers, today the highlight is the homemade apple pies prepared by the town's women and sold by the slice. The most exciting part about this tradition comes with a revelation of the nature of pie making: Although they are all double-crusted wedges resplendent with fresh fall apples, no two pies are alike! Their uniqueness lies in the type of apples chosen, the combination of spices, and the hands that prepare the crust. Keeping this in mind, the combination of ingredients I put forth here is my favorite. I hope this will encourage you to develop your own. This recipe may be prepared in a 9-inch pie plate; however, for a more dramatic presentation, I prefer to use a 2-inch-deep, 8-inch-round fluted tart pan with a removable bottom.

Pie

   1 batch Pastry dough (page 226)

   8 large baking apples

   1 teaspoon ground cinnamon

   ¼ cup date sugar, honey, or maple syrup

   2 tablespoons unbleached all-purpose flour

   4 teaspoons unsalted butter, cut into bits

Egg glaze

   1 large egg yolk

   4 to 5 drops water

Have ready one 9-inch pie plate or one 2-inch-deep, 8-inch-round fluted tart pan.

   Use two-thirds of the pastry dough to line the tart or pie pan. To prevent an uncooked, soggy crust, I always blind bake the crust (see box, page 157). Roll out the remaining dough and slice it into enough strips to create a lattice top. Place the strips in an airtight container or wrap them well in plastic wrap and refrigerate until you are ready to finish preparing the pie.

Position the oven rack on the lowest level. Preheat the oven to 375°F.

Peel and core the apples and slice them into ⅓-inch-thick wedges. In a large bowl, toss them with the cinnamon, your choice of sweetener, and the flour.

Put the apples into the prepared crust. Dot with the butter. Working quickly, create a lattice top with the pastry strips.

To prepare the glaze, in a small bowl, mix the egg yolk with 4 to 5 drops of water. Brush the lattice top with the egg glaze.

Bake for 45 minutes to 1 hour, or until the apples have cooked through and the juice boils. If the top crust begins to brown too quickly, cover with aluminum foil which has been pierced with a fork to allow the steam to escape. Serve warm or chilled.

Comparing Apples to Apples

When choosing apples for pies and cakes, keep in mind you want a variety of apple that will hold its shape, without producing too much juice, such as Northern Spy, Golden Delicious, Granny Smith, or Cortland. For sauces and sorbets, soft apples are desirable; select varieties such as Macintosh or Ida Red.

Banana Cream Tart with Dark Chocolate Sauce

Makes one 10-inch-round tart; 8 servings

These days, one rarely finds banana cream pie on a restaurant menu, but every time I mention it, people immediately smile.

Pastry

1 batch Sweet Tart Pastry (page 233)

Banana cream filling

2 cups chilled whole milk

1 teaspoon unflavored gelatin

1 large egg

2 large egg yolks

3 tablespoons cornstarch

¼ cup honey

1 tablespoon pure vanilla extract

1½ cups heavy cream

2 large ripe bananas

Sauce

1 batch Dark Chocolate Sauce (page 218)

Prepare and bake the Sweet Tart Pastry recipe following the instructions on page 157 to make one 10-inch-round tart shell. Let the pastry shell cool completely before filling.

To make the banana cream filling, pour about ½ cup of the chilled milk into a small bowl. Sprinkle the gelatin over the milk and let it soften while you prepare the other ingredients.

In a medium bowl, combine the egg, egg yolks, cornstarch, and honey, and whisk until thoroughly blended. Mix in the softened gelatin.

Into a large saucepan, pour the remaining milk and bring it to a boil. To prevent the egg mixture from curdling, gradually add to it the boiled milk, whisking constantly. Transfer the milk mixture to a clean saucepan. Stirring constantly, cook the mixture over medium heat until it comes to a boil. Continue to cook for 2 minutes. Immediately remove the pan from the heat and pass the mixture through a strainer set over a clean bowl. Stir in the vanilla extract.

Cover the custard with plastic wrap pressed to the surface. Refrigerate until chilled, but not set, about 30 minutes. When the custard is chilled, whip the heavy cream until soft peaks form in a chilled, large bowl. Fold 1 cup of the whipped cream into the custard.

Thinly slice the bananas and fold them into the custard. Pour the banana custard into the tart shell. Chill the tart until the custard is set, about 3 hours. To decorate the tart, pipe the remaining whipped cream over the top of the custard.

To serve, drizzle the chocolate sauce on each dessert plate. Slice the tart into 8 wedges and place the slice on top of the sauce. Watch everyone smile!

Note: Since the bananas will begin to color as soon as they are [peel]ed, it is best [to] serve the tart [th]e same day it is prepared.

Blueberry Gooseberry Crumb Pie

Makes one 10-inch pie; 8 servings

Sweet blueberries work well with the tangy flavor of gooseberries. Liquid FruitSource provides just enough sweetener without masking the flavor of the berries. Make sure the fruit bubbles, allowing the sweetener to blend with the juices of the fruit.

Pie

1 batch Pastry (page 226)

3 cups fresh blueberries, rinsed and stemmed (wild, if available)

1 cup gooseberries, rinsed and stemmed

1 teaspoon ground cinnamon

2 tablespoons unbleached all-purpose flour

¼ cup liquid FruitSource (see Note, page 71)

2 tablespoons unsalted butter, chilled

Crumb topping

1⅓ cups unbleached all-purpose flour

⅓ cup maple sugar

¼ teaspoon ground cinnamon

½ cup (1 stick) unsalted butter, melted

Prepare the pastry following the instructions on page 226 to line one 10-inch tart pan with a removable bottom. Freeze any leftover dough. Blind bake the tart until the inside of the shell is lightly browned (see box, page 157). Let the shell cool.

Position the oven rack in the bottom of the oven. Preheat the oven to 375°F.

In a large bowl, combine the blueberries, gooseberries, cinnamon, and flour. Pour in the FruitSource and mix to coat all of the berries. Spread the fruit mixture into the prepared tart shell. Dot with the chilled butter.

To make the crumb topping, in a clean, medium bowl, combine the flour, maple sugar, and cinnamon. Pour in the melted

Note: To prevent the tart from becoming too brown, after the tart has baked for 30 minutes, place a piece of aluminum foil over the top. Pierce the foil with a fork to allow the steam to escape and continue baking as directed.

butter. Using either a wooden spoon or your hands, rub the ingredients together to form crumbs. Sprinkle the crumbs over the fruit.

Bake for about 55 minutes or until the juices begin to bubble (see Note). Cool. To serve, slice into 8 wedges.

Blind Baking

To blind bake a tart or pie shell, prick the crust with the tines of a fork in several places. Place a piece of aluminum foil or parchment paper over the shell and fill with pastry weights, rice, or beans. If blind baking small or mini-tart shells, use paper muffin cups to line the inside. Bake in the lower part of the oven for about 15 minutes. Remove the weights and the aluminum foil and return the shell to the oven. Place it on the middle rack and bake for 5 to 10 minutes or until the center is lightly browned. If the pastry will be baked after it is filled, such as in the case of a fruit pie, it may not be necessary to brown the center thoroughly.

However, if the recipe calls for a baked shell, make sure the pastry is completely baked through.

Blueberry Pie

Makes one 10-inch pie; 8 servings

Sweet, wild blueberries are a sure sign of summer. I like to top this pie with a lattice crust to show off the intense midnight-blue color of the berries, and I often use uneven-sized strips of pastry for the lattice work. FruitSource will sweeten, but not mask, the flavor of the berries. Make sure the fruit bubbles, allowing the sweetener to blend with the juices of the fruit.

Pie

> 1 batch Pastry (page 226)
> 4 cups fresh blueberries, rinsed and stemmed (wild if available)
> 1 teaspoon ground cinnamon
> 2 tablespoons unbleached all-purpose flour
> 2 teaspoons lemon zest, finely chopped
> ¼ cup liquid FruitSource (see Note, page 71)
> 2 tablespoons unsalted butter, chilled

Egg glaze

> 1 egg yolk
> Water

Note: To prevent the top crust from becoming too brown, place a piece of aluminum fo over the top. Pierce the foi with a fork t allow the stea to escape and continue baking as directed.

Prepare the pastry following the instructions on page 226 to line one 10-inch tart pan with a removable bottom, and to make strips for a lattice top. Keep the strips chilled in an airtight container or plastic wrap until ready to use. Blind bake the tart until the inside of the shell is lightly browned. Cool.

Position the oven rack in the bottom of the oven. Preheat the oven to 375°F.

In a large bowl, combine the blueberries, cinnamon, flour, and lemon zest. Pour in the FruitSource and mix to coat the berries. Spread the fruit mixture into the prepared tart shell. Dot with the chilled butter. Use the strips of pastry to weave a lattice top over the fruit.

To make the egg glaze, combine the egg yolk with a few drops of water in a small bowl. Brush the lattice top with the glaze. Bake for about 55 minutes or until the juices begin to bubble. Cool.

Butter Tarts

Makes 24 mini-tarts

Butter tarts are Canada's answer to America's pecan pie, but without the pecans. Some people add raisins, others prefer nuts. The real debate is whether you prefer the filling firm or runny. This recipe produces a rich, firm filling which works well with nuts or raisins or just by itself.

1 batch Pastry (page 226)
¼ cup organic Thompson dark raisins (optional)
¼ cup chopped walnuts (optional)
¼ cup (½ stick) unsalted butter, at room temperature
½ cup maple sugar
½ cup honey
2 large eggs
2 teaspoons pure vanilla extract
1 tablespoon apple cider vinegar
Pinch of salt

Preheat the oven to 375°F. Butter two 12 mini-sized muffin tins.

Roll out the pastry dough to ⅛ inch thick. Cut dough into circles with a biscuit cutter or a glass to fit the muffin cups and line the cups with the dough. Chill the prepared pan until ready to fill.

Distribute the raisins and walnuts among the tart shells. In a medium bowl, cream the butter and the maple sugar until light. Beat in the honey, eggs, vanilla extract, cider vinegar, and salt. Immediately spoon the honey mixture into the prepared muffin cups, filling the cups two-thirds full. Bake for about 25 minutes. Make sure the pastry is golden brown. As the tarts bake, the tops will become dark brown. Cool tarts on a wire rack.

Butternut Squash Tarts

Makes 8 tarts

Squash is highly versatile because it goes well in both savory and sweet dishes. Each type of squash has a unique texture and flavor, some fuller than others. I have limited the amount of spices so that the light flavor of the butternut squash can come through.

> 1 medium butternut squash, about 2 pounds
> 1 batch Pastry (page 226)
> 3 large eggs
> 1 cup half-and-half
> ⅓ cup brown rice syrup
> 1½ teaspoons ground cinnamon
> ½ teaspoon freshly ground nutmeg
> Pinch of freshly ground black pepper
> ½ teaspoon salt

Preheat the oven to 400°F. Bake the squash until tender, about 45 minutes. When it is cool enough to handle, peel and remove the seeds of the squash. Purée the flesh in a blender or food processor. There will be about 2 cups.

Prepare the pastry according to the directions on page 226 to line eight 4½-inch-round tart pans with removable bottoms. Blind bake. Remove the pastry shells from the oven and let cool. Reduce the oven temperature to 350°F.

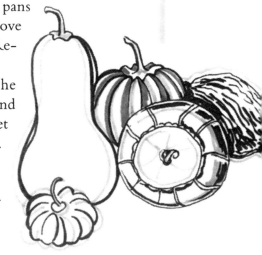

In the food processor, mix together the squash purée, eggs, cream, brown rice syrup, and the spices. Put the shells on a large baking sheet and fill each tart shell with the squash mixture. Bake the tarts for about 20 minutes or until the centers have risen and the filling has set.

Let cool. Serve at room temperature or chilled.

Squashing the Squash

If you have ever tried to cut through the tough flesh of a raw squash, you will know it can be quite frustrating. But here is a way to squash the frustration of the squash! A friend had to convince me she was right about knowing a great way to bake squash. It turned out to be the easiest and most flavorful way I have found to cook squash that will later be mashed or puréed. Just put the entire squash in the oven and bake until it is tender. The squash steams as it bakes. The skin will loosen itself and all of the sweetness remains contained in the flesh. When the squash is cool enough to handle, separate the skin from the flesh. Cut the cooked squash in half and scoop out the seeds.

Remember, you can bake it in advance and keep it refrigerated or frozen until you are ready to use it.

Chocolate Coconut Cream Pie

Makes one 10-inch tart; 8 servings

The rum-flavored coconut custard is cradled by the dark, bittersweet chocolate pastry. I like to drizzle melted semi-sweet chocolate over the top to create an even more striking visual effect.

Pastry

1 batch Chocolate Pastry (page 214)

1 large egg white

Coconut filling

1 cup *crème fraîche* (see box, page 163)

3 large eggs

⅓ cup brown rice syrup

¼ cup dark rum

Pinch of salt

Pinch of cinnamon

3 cups shredded unsweetened coconut

Decoration

¼ cup semi-sweet grain-sweetened chocolate chips (see Note, page 101), melted

Sauce

¾ cup semi-sweet grain-sweetened chocolate chips (see Note, page 101)

¾ cup unsweetened coconut milk

Prepare and bake the chocolate pastry following the instructions on page 214 to make one 10-inch tart shell. When the pastry shell is cool, brush the inside lightly with the egg white.

Preheat the oven to 375°F.

In a large bowl, whisk together the *crème fraîche*, eggs, brown rice syrup, rum, salt, and cinnamon. Mix in the coconut. Pour the coconut mixture into the baked pastry shell and bake for about 30 minutes or until the custard has set and the top is very lightly browned. Let cool for 15 minutes.

To decorate the tart, dip a fork into the melted chips to drizzle thin lines of the chocolate across the top.

To make the chocolate coconut sauce, melt the chocolate chips in a bowl set over a pan of simmering water. When melted, stir in the coconut milk. The sauce may be made in advance, but it will thicken as it cools. To serve, rewarm.

Serve the tart at room temperature. Drizzle some of the warm sauce over each plate and top each slice with a dollop of whipped cream. Refrigerate any leftover slices.

Crème Fraîche

Crème fraîche is a French version of sour cream only with a more subtle flavor, because it is made from unpasteurized cream. It is easy to simulate. In a nonreactive bowl, combine 1 cup of heavy cream (35 percent butter fat) with 2 tablespoons of sour cream. Cover with plastic wrap and leave it at room temperature overnight. Stir and refrigerate until ready to use. It will keep for about 5 days. (Makes 1 cup.)

Chocolate Pecan Pie

Makes one 10-inch pie; 8 servings

If you have a real sweet tooth, try sinking your teeth into the smooth, chocolatey filling, the crunchy pecan topping, and the rich, flaky pastry of this pie.

1 batch Pastry (see page 226)

½ cup semi-sweet grain-sweetened chocolate chips (see Note, page 101)

2 tablespoons unsalted butter

1 cup maple sugar

1 cup brown rice syrup

3 large eggs

1 teaspoon pure vanilla extract

Pinch of salt

1½ cups pecan halves

Preheat the oven to 375°F.

Prepare the pastry following the recipe on page 226 to make one blind baked, 10-inch tart shell. (For instructions on blind baking, see box, page 157.)

Melt the chocolate chips and butter in a small bowl set over simmering water.

In a large bowl, mix together the maple sugar, brown rice syrup, eggs, vanilla extract, and salt. Beat in the melted chocolate and butter mixture. Mix in the pecans. Pour the mixture into the blind baked shell.

Bake for about 45 minutes. The center should rise. If you prefer a runny filling, make sure the shell is well baked prior to filling and remove the pie from the oven once the center has risen, about 45 minutes. For a firmer filling, let the center fall before removing from the oven; bake for about 15 minutes more.

Chocolate–Pine Nut Tart

Makes one 8 x 11-inch tart; 8 servings

For people who like their chocolate in different textures, this tart has a creamy filling encased by a bittersweet chocolate pastry. The rich pine nuts provide the crunch. I like to make this in a rectangular tart pan, but one 10-inch-round pan works just as well.

Pastry

> 1 batch Chocolate Pastry (page 214)

Filling

> 1 cup pine nuts
>
> ½ cup semi-sweet grain-sweetened chocolate chips (see Note, page 101)
>
> 1 cup heavy cream
>
> 2 large eggs
>
> 2 tablespoons brown rice syrup
>
> ½ teaspoon pure vanilla extract

Preheat the oven to 350°F.

Prepare the pastry following the instructions on page 214 to line one 18 × 11–inch tart pan with a removable bottom. Bake the pastry for 15 minutes. Let cool.

Spread the pine nuts on a baking sheet and toast in the oven until lightly golden, about 5 minutes. Watch carefully, because the nuts will burn very easily. Let cool.

In a medium bowl set over simmering water, melt the chocolate chips. Remove the bowl from the heat and stir in the cream. Add the eggs, rice syrup, and vanilla and whisk together until completely blended. Stir in the pine nuts.

Pour the mixture into the baked pastry shell and bake for 25 minutes. The center will rise before the baking time is up, but continue to bake until the edges of the filling crack. The filling will remain creamy, but it will deflate as soon as it is removed from the oven. Let cool. Serve at room temperature.

Double Sour Cherry Tarts

Makes six 4-inch tarts

My brother Sheldon has always had an affinity to cherry pie. It started with Hostess, but I hope it ends here. Sour cherries have a very short season, so take advantage of them while you can. Serve these tarts with sour cherry sauce for double the taste.

Pastry

> 1 batch Pastry (page 226)
>
> 6 tablespoons maple butter

Fruit filling

> 3 cups pitted sour cherries
>
> 2 tablespoons unbleached all-purpose flour
>
> 1 teaspoon ground cinnamon
>
> 1 teaspoon lemon zest, finely chopped
>
> 2 tablespoons unsalted butter, chilled and chopped into small pieces

Egg glaze

> 1 large egg yolk
>
> Water

Sauce

> 1 batch Sour Cherry Sauce (page 230)

Using two-thirds of the pastry dough, line six 4-inch-round tart pans with removable bottoms. Freeze for at least 10 minutes, or until ready to bake. Reserve the leftover dough in the refrigerator to make strips for the lattice top.

Position the oven rack in the bottom of the oven. Preheat the oven to 400°F. Blind bake the crust until the inside is lightly browned. (See page 157 for directions on blind baking.) Let cool. Spread 1 tablespoon of the maple butter in the bottom of each tart shell.

In a bowl, toss the cherries with the flour, cinnamon, zest, and butter. Fill each tart shell with about ½ cup of the cherry mixture.

Roll the reserved dough on a lightly floured work surface to ⅛-inch thick and cut into ⅓-inch-wide strips. Weave strips to form a lattice top over each tart. If the dough is getting too soft, refrigerate the tarts for 5 minutes before proceeding. To make the egg glaze, combine the egg yolk with a few drops of water in a small cup. Brush the lattice top with the egg glaze.

Place the tarts in the oven on the bottom rack. Reduce the oven temperature to 375°F and bake for about 40 minutes, or until the pastry is golden brown and the juice from the cherries begins to bubble. Let cool for 5 minutes. Carefully remove the tarts from the pan and slide them onto a wire rack to cool.

Serve the tarts with the Sour Cherry Sauce (page 230) on the side.

Fig and Frangipane Tarts

Makes 6 tarts

Fresh figs take only a few minutes to cook, which makes them a perfect topping for the frangipane. If you don't want to spend the time to fuss with tart pans, they can be made into freeform galettes. Follow the instructions for the Rhubarb Galette on page 176, substituting the frangipane for the maple butter and almond mixture.

> **1 batch Pastry (page 226)**
> **1 batch Hazelnut Frangipane (page 221)**
> **12 fresh figs**

Preheat the oven to 400℉.

Prepare the pastry following the instructions on page 157 to line six 4 × ½-inch-round tart pans with removable bottoms. Freeze any leftover dough. Blind bake the tart shells until the insides are lightly browned in the preheated oven. Let cool.

Preheat the oven to 375℉.

Fill the shells with the Hazelnut Frangipane. Cut the figs into quarters lengthwise. Using 2 figs for each tart, in a circle pattern, place 8 pieces of the figs on top of the frangipane. Bake for about 15 minutes, or until the frangipane has risen and is lightly browned. Let cool before serving.

Note: If maing galettes, baking time will increase by 5 to 10 minutes. M sure the bott of the crust well browned

Lemon Meringue Pie

Makes 10 servings

This lemon meringue pie is worth the effort. You can prepare the lemon curd three days in advance, bake the tart shell the day before, and then all you have to prepare the day you will serve it is the meringue.

Meringue

    4 large egg whites, at room temperature
    Pinch of salt
    ¼ teaspoon cream of tartar
    1¼ cups maple syrup
    ¼ cup water

Pie

    1 batch Lemon Tart (page 170)

Preheat the oven to 450°F.

    In the large bowl of an electric mixer, at medium-slow speed, begin beating the egg whites until they are foamy. Add the salt and the cream of tartar. Gradually increase the machine speed to medium-fast and continue beating the egg whites until stiff, shiny peaks are formed, making sure to not overbeat.

    In a medium saucepan, bring the syrup and water to a boil over high heat. Continue boiling until the syrup reaches just past the soft ball stage, 242°F on a candy thermometer. Or place a few drops of syrup in the water; the syrup should harden but remain pliable.

    With the mixer speed on slow, dribble the syrup into the beaten egg whites. Increase the speed of the mixer and continue beating until the egg whites become cool, and form stiff, upright peaks, 15 to 20 minutes.

    Spread the meringue over the warm lemon tart making sure not to leave any gaps between the meringue and the crust (see Note). Use a fork or a cake comb to make a pattern in the meringue. Bake for about 10 minutes or until golden brown, watching carefully not to overbake.

Note: It is best to spread the meringue on a warm base. To do this, prepare the lemon tart so you bake the filling just before you plan to finish it with the meringue.

Lemon Tart

Makes 10 servings

This is a rich, luscious, and tart tart! For convenience, make the filling in advance.

Pastry
1 batch Pastry (page 226)

Lemon curd
6 large eggs
2 large egg yolks
1 scant cup maple syrup
½ cup plus 2 tablespoons freshly squeezed lemon juice
½ cup (1 stick) unsalted butter, cut into ½-inch chunks
Zest of 2 lemons, finely chopped

Preheat the oven to 400°F.

Use two-thirds of the dough to line one 10-inch tart pan with a removable bottom. Freeze any leftover pastry. Fully bake the shell in the preheated oven until it is golden brown. Let cool.

In a large stainless steel bowl, use a whisk to combine the eggs, egg yolks, maple syrup, and lemon juice. Add the butter and set the bowl over a pot of simmering water. Whisking constantly, cook the mixture until it becomes very thick, being careful not to let the mixture come to a boil. It should take about 8 minutes for it to thicken once it has become hot to the touch. Immediately remove the bowl from the simmering water and pour the mixture through a strainer set over a clean bowl. Stir in the lemon zest. Cover the mixture with plastic wrap pressed to its surface to prevent a skin from forming. Let cool.

Preheat the oven to 375°F.

Pour the lemon curd into the baked tart shell and bake in the middle of the oven for 15 to 20 minutes or until the filling is set and very lightly browned.

Note: The filling can be prepared up t 3 days in advance and refrigerated until ready to use.

Pastry: Wet or Dry?

I used to think the drier the pie dough, the better. I still think it is better that the dough be a little drier rather than sticky, but in either case there is no need to be afraid to make some adjustments. Your goal is to create a pliable dough without too much handling or kneading. The flour will absorb some of the moisture as the dough rests, but if it is crumbling all over as you attempt to wrap it in the plastic, sprinkle a few more drops of water into the dough. Pat it together. On the other hand, if the dough is too sticky, sprinkle it with a little flour. In either case, let the dough rest in the refrigerate for at least 1 hour.

Blind bake according to recipe requirements.

Pear-Ginger Strudel

Makes 1 strudel; 6 servings

Honey- and ginger-infused pears surrounded by layers of crisp, buttery phyllo pastry make a quick and delicious substitute for a traditional dessert. Although the pears require some preplanning, they may be poached days in advanced. The strudel can be assembled earlier during the day you plan to serve it, then baked while your guests are eating their entrées. Serve it warm from the oven for a memorable finish.

> **1 batch Honey Poached Apricots (page 49)**
> **3 tablespoons reserved poaching liquid**
> **1 teaspoon cornstarch**
> **¼ teaspoon ground ginger**
> **Pinch of freshly grated nutmeg**
> **6 sheets phyllo pastry**
> **⅓ cup unsalted butter, melted**

Preheat the oven to 375°F. Have ready a cookie sheet.

Slice the pears into ½-inch-thick wedges. Put in a small bowl and toss with the poaching liquid, cornstarch, ginger, and nutmeg.

Use the melted butter to prepare the phyllo sheets, according to the instructions for working with phyllo on page 174. To make the phyllo into a strudel, cut a piece of parchment paper to fit the size of your baking sheet. The paper will be used to help shape the strudel and to transfer the strudel to the baking pan as well as a nonstick surface during the baking.

Place the buttered phyllo sheets on the parchment paper in a stack. Starting at the edge closer to you, spoon the pears onto the sheet, leaving about 1 inch at either end. Mound the pears as much as possible rather than letting them spread out.

To create a log, carefully lift the closest edge of the parchment paper while rolling the pastry over the filling. Let go of the paper and continue rolling the pastry until all the filling is encased, finishing with the seam side down. Press the open ends together and fold them securely underneath the log.

Position the log on the paper and use the paper to transfer the strudel to the cookie sheet. Place the strudel on the paper in the center of the pan. To allow for the steam to escape while baking, use a sharp knife to make 3 to 4 slashes on the diagonal along the top of the log. Bake for 25 to 35 minutes, or until the top and the bottom is golden brown and the liquid has begun to bubble. If the top begins to brown too quickly, cover loosely with aluminum foil. Remove the strudel from the oven and slide a wire rack underneath it.

Slice the strudel on the diagonal. Serve warm or at room temperature. Serve each piece with some of the poaching liquid and a dollop of Lemon Whipped Cream (page 91).

Phyllo

Phyllo refers to paper-thin sheets of pastry dough usually found in groceries specializing in Greek foods, Middle Eastern markets, and at some supermarkets. The standard size is 18¼ × 11½-inches and these usually come in a box with 16 sheets. When working with phyllo, the most important thing is to prevent the sheets from drying out. Use a spray bottle to spritz 2 dish towels with just enough water to dampen them lightly. Sandwich the phyllo sheets between the two towels making sure none of the pastry is exposed. The moisture in the towels will keep the phyllo from drying out. If the towels are too damp, the pastry touching the towels will become wet. In this case, create a barrier layer between the pastry and the damp towels with waxed paper or plastic wrap.

Work with one sheet at a time; remove the sheet, and carefully replace the top towel over the other sheets. To coat the sheets with butter, brush one side of the sheet with warm, melted butter. Turn the sheet over and repeat. Lay the next sheet on top of the first sheet and only brush the exposed side with butter. Repeat with the remaining sheets.

Chocolate-Walnut Cigars

Makes 8 cigars

This is a very quick dessert that has a surprising flavor combination. These can be served either individually or as part of an assortment of sweets. Cut the cigars into thirds for bite-sized pieces.

> 1 cup semi-sweet grain-sweetened chocolate chips (see Note, page 101)
>
> ½ cup walnuts, chopped
>
> ½ teaspoon ground cinnamon
>
> 8 sheets phyllo pastry
>
> ½ cup (1 stick) unsalted butter, melted
>
> 3 to 4 tablespoons honey

Preheat the oven to 375°F. Butter or line a cookie sheet with parchment paper.

In a small bowl, combine the chocolate, walnuts, and cinnamon.

Working with the phyllo as described on page 174, position the long side of the pastry horizontally and brush the right half of the pastry with the melted butter. Fold in half, folding the left side of the phyllo over the buttered half, pressing down the folded edge. You should now have a rectangle with the shorter side positioned horizontally. Brush the top and bottom liberally with butter. Working with the edge closest to you, spread one-eighth of the chocolate mixture along the edge, leaving about a 1-inch border on either end. Drizzle about 1 teaspoon of the honey over the chocolate filling.

To prevent the chocolate mixture from coming out of the ends of the cigar, fold the outer edges of the phyllo over the ends of chocolate. Continue folding the edges along the entire length of the pastry. To form the cigar, roll the pastry over the chocolate encasing it in the phyllo. As you roll make sure the folded edges remain tucked in.

Place the cigar on the prepared cookie sheet, seam side down, and brush with extra melted butter. Repeat with the remaining ingredients to produce 8 cigars. Bake for about 10 minutes or until the pastry is golden brown all over. Serve warm.

Rhubarb Galette

Makes one 12-inch tart; 8 servings

When choosing rhubarb, look for intensely red-colored, young stalks. If only large stalks are available, use a vegetable peeler to remove the outer layer to eliminate the chance of biting into any overly fibrous pieces. The high water content of the rhubarb creates a lot of juice when it is cooked; therefore, maple butter is a great way to sweeten this pastry without creating additional liquid.

This free-form tart is a quick way to create an elegant dessert in a pinch.

Pastry

1 batch Pastry (page 226)

Fruit filling

4 stalks rhubarb, cut into ¾-inch-long chunks (about 4 cups)

1 tablespoon orange zest, finely chopped

¼ cup unbleached all-purpose flour

¼ cup finely ground blanched almonds

2 tablespoons unsalted butter, chilled

¼ cup plus 1 tablespoon maple butter

Egg glaze

1 large egg yolk

Water

Topping

¼ cup sliced almonds

Line a baking sheet with parchment paper. Position the oven rack in the bottom of the oven. Preheat the oven to 400°F.

Using two-thirds of the pastry dough, on a lightly floured work surface, roll out the dough to ⅛-inch thick, forming a circle approximately 16 inches in diameter. Do not trim the edges. Transfer the dough to the prepared baking sheet and refrigerate.

In a bowl, toss the rhubarb with the orange zest. In another bowl, combine the flour and the ground almonds. Cut in the butter until the mixture resembles coarse meal.

Spread the maple butter over the crust, leaving a 4-inch-wide border around the circumference of the circle. Sprinkle the flour mixture over the maple butter. Pile the rhubarb over the flour mixture. To create sides, carefully gather the edges of the dough, up and over the rhubarb, folding the dough towards the center of the circle, leaving a 6-inch-round gap in the center. Pleat the dough at the top as necessary to encase the filling. Once secure, refrigerate the galette for 10 minutes.

In a small cup, beat the egg yolk and a few drops of water together to make the egg glaze. Brush the top of the galette with the egg glaze. Before the glaze dries, sprinkle the sliced almonds in a circle around the center opening. Bake on the bottom rack for 20 minutes. Reduce the temperature to 375°F and continue baking for about 25 minutes, or until the tart is deep brown on the top and bottom and the juice from the rhubarb is bubbling. Remove from the oven and carefully slide a wire rack under the tart. Cool. Serve warm or at room temperature.

Roasted Plum and Ginger Strudel

Makes 6 servings

The flavor and color of the plums will be intensified by the roasting process, and the juice will thicken naturally as it cools. The ginger subtly envelops the fruit in the buttery layers of phyllo.

Filling

   3½ pounds ripe, firm red or black plums

   ½ cup maple sugar

   1 tablespoon orange zest, finely chopped

   ½ teaspoon ground ginger

Pastry

   6 tablespoons granular FruitSource (see Note, page 71)

   1½ teaspoons ground ginger

   6 sheets phyllo pastry

   ½ cup (1 stick) unsalted butter, melted

Preheat the oven to 400°F.

Cut the plums into quarters, removing the stones, and place in a 9 × 13-inch glass baking dish. Toss with the maple sugar. Bake for about 30 minutes, or until the plums soften and the juices bubble. Let cool completely. Gently mix the plums with the orange zest and ginger. The recipe may be prepared up to this point the day before. If so, refrigerate the filling until ready to use.

To prepare the strudel, preheat the oven to 350°F. Line a baking sheet with parchment paper.

In a small bowl, combine the FruitSource with the ginger. Working with one sheet of phyllo at a time, and following the instruction on page 174, brush half of the sheet with butter. Sprinkle one-sixth of the FruitSource and ginger mixture over the buttered half. Fold the phyllo over the buttered half. Brush butter on the top and bottom sides of the phyllo. Working with the narrow edge closer to you, spoon one-sixth of the plum mixture onto the phyllo, leaving about a 1-inch-wide border on either end. Fold over the borders along the entire length of the pastry. Roll the pastry over the plums, loosely encasing them in the phyllo, and as you roll, making sure the folded edges remain tucked in. End with the seam side down.

Transfer to the prepared baking sheet. Brush the top with extra butter. Score the top with 2 diagonal slashes to allow steam to escape. Repeat with the remaining ingredients to produce 6 individual strudels. Bake until the pastry is golden brown on top and bottom, about 15 minutes. Transfer to a wire rack. Serve warm.

Walnut Baklava

Makes 12 triangles

Baklava is one of those desserts you would rarely think of preparing yourself. However, it is quite easy to make and it works really well with natural syrups. To allow for the pastry to absorb the syrup, it is best to prepare the baklava 48 hours before you plan to serve it.

Nut filling
½ pound of walnuts, finely chopped
1 teaspoon ground cinnamon
¼ cup date sugar
5 sheets phyllo pastry
1 cup (2 sticks) unsalted butter, melted

Syrup
⅔ cup maple syrup
⅔ cup brown rice syrup
Pinch of ground cloves
3 tablespoons freshly squeezed lemon juice
½ teaspoon pure vanilla extract

Preheat the oven to 325°F. Butter one 9 × 6-inch nonreactive baking dish, preferably clear glass.

In a small bowl, combine the finely chopped walnuts, cinnamon, and date sugar.

Working with the phyllo as described on page 174, cut the sheets into quarters. Using the melted butter, brush one quarter of the sheet and place it in the baking dish. Repeat with six more quarters, piling them on top of one another. Spread one-third of the nut mixture over the last buttered quarter that is in the dish. Butter another quarter and place it over the nuts. Spread another third of the nut mixture over the last layer of buttered phyllo. Repeat until all of the nut mixture has been used. Then butter the remaining phyllo sheets and layer them over the last layer of the nut mixture.

Use a sharp knife to cut the pastry into triangular pieces. Begin by cutting the top of the pastry cross-wise into thirds, cutting through to the deepest layer of the nut filling. Then cut each third in half horizontally, creating squares. Cut each square diagonally.

Bake for about 45 minutes or until the pastry is thoroughly golden brown.

Prepare the syrup just prior to removing the pastry from the oven. In a small nonreactive saucepan, combine the maple syrup and the brown rice syrup. Set over medium-low heat. When the mixture is hot, add the cloves, lemon juice, and vanilla extract. Continue cooking for about 5 minutes. When the pastry is out of the oven, pour half of the syrup over the top. Let it rest for 30 minutes. Pour the remaining syrup over the top. Cover with plastic wrap and let the baklava sit for at least 48 hours at room temperature. Cut into triangles and serve at room temperature.

Chapter Eight

SOMETHING DIFFERENT

*a*s the title suggests, this chapter contains a collection of desserts for those times when you want to serve something a little different. Some use a collection of recipes from the components chapter, like the Lime Trifle which calls for Genoise, Lime Curd, and Blueberry Sauce, while others are just unique, like the Banana Caramel Pecan Fritters. There are recipes for steam puddings and snacks. Others are variations on more common recipes, such as the array of Chocolate Crêpes recipes. But no matter which recipes you decide to prepare, they are all sure to become a part of your dessert repertoire.

Apple Fritters

Makes 4 servings

The role location plays in the enjoyment of food is amazing. If you were sitting in an expensive restaurant and were presented with a large plate of freshly made apple fritters garnished with quenelles of cinnamon ice cream, you would be oohing and aahing about the brilliant innovation. If you were at the local farmers' market, eating freshly made apple fritters, you would probably be nostalgic for simpler times. Whichever setting you prefer, your taste buds will thank you for making this recipe. Remember, anything fried is best served immediately. Don't forget the ice cream!

Batter

- 2 large egg yolks
- ⅔ cup milk
- 1 tablespoon honey
- 1 tablespoon unsalted butter, melted
- 1 cup unbleached all-purpose flour
- ¼ teaspoon salt
- ¼ teaspoon freshly grated nutmeg
- About 1 quart of vegetable oil for deep frying
- 2 large egg whites, at room temperature

Fruit

- 4 medium baking apples (see box, page 153)

Garnish

- ½ cup maple sugar
- 1 teaspoon ground cinnamon

In a small bowl, mix together the egg yolks, milk, honey, melted butter, flour, salt, and nutmeg until smooth. Cover with plastic wrap and let rest for at least 2 hours.

Either in a deep fryer or in a deep, heavy 3-quart saucepan, heat the oil to a constant 375°F on a frying thermometer. Or test by dropping about 1 teaspoon of batter into the hot oil. The oil should immediately sizzle around the batter. (If the oil begins to smoke, it is too hot, and you should reduce the heat.)

In a clean bowl of an electric mixer, beat the egg whites until firm, but not dry. Fold into the batter.

Peel and core the apples. To prevent discoloration, work with one apple at a time. Cut the apple crosswise into rings about ¼-inch thick. When the oil has reached the proper temperature, working with one slice at a time, coat the apple slice with the batter allowing the excess to drip off. Gently slide the coated slice into the hot oil. Without crowding the pot, add additional slices. Cook until golden brown, turning as the underside browns. Use tongs to remove the fritters from the oil and pat gently on paper towels to eliminate any excess oil. Let rest on a wire rack set over paper towels to catch any excess oil. Work quickly to prepare the remaining apples.

In a small bowl, mix together the maple sugar and cinnamon. To serve, dip each slice into the cinnamon sugar as you position the slices on the serving plate. Serve immediately.

Black Forest Crêpes

Makes 6 servings

This is the land of Black Forest Cake revisited. I've taken the main components—chocolate, cherries, and whipped cream—and assembled them with a bit of a twist.

Clarified butter (page 189) for frying
12 Chocolate Crêpes (page 213)
1½ cups heavy cream
1 teaspoon pure vanilla extract
1 recipe Dark Chocolate Sauce (page 218)
1 recipe Sour Cherry Sauce (page 230)
Unsweetened cocoa powder for garnish

Warm individual dessert plates and line one large serving plate with parchment paper.

Into a heavy frying pan, pour some clarified butter and set over medium heat. Place 1 crêpe into the pan and heat on both sides, until warm to the touch, about 2 minutes per side. Working quickly, with tongs, fold the crêpe in half and then into quarters. Place on the parchment-lined plate and keep warm in a 150°F oven while you heat the remaining crêpes.

Meanwhile, in a chilled bowl, whip the heavy cream with the vanilla extract until soft peaks form.

Just before serving, heat both the chocolate sauce and the cherry sauce in small saucepans over low heat until warm to the touch, about 3 minutes. To assemble, place two folded crêpes on each plate. Drizzle the warm chocolate sauce in a circle over the crêpes and the plate. Spoon the cherry sauce and dark chocolate sauce over the crêpes and top with a large dollop of whipped cream. Sprinkle the plates with a dusting of cocoa powder. Serve immediately.

Apple-Rosemary Pizza

Makes 1 pizza; 8 servings

The inspiration for this recipe came when I was teaching a six-hour yeast-bread workshop at the French Culinary Institute in New York City. It was a one-day class and I wanted to expose the students to a variety of techniques for working with yeast. Most importantly, I wanted them to learn not to be intimidated by the yeast. Together we experimented with a savory pizza recipe I had made hundreds of times, exchanging ingredients for dessert flavors while maintaining the same proportions. To everyone's surprise, it was a glowing success.

Dough

2 tablespoons warm water

1 scant tablespoon dry active yeast

½ cup milk, at room temperature

1 tablespoon honey

1 tablespoon unsalted butter, at room temperature

2 cups unbleached all-purpose flour

½ teaspoon salt

Cornmeal for preparing the pan

Topping

¼ cup (½ stick) unsalted butter

4 firm large apples, peeled and cored (see box, page 153)

2 teaspoons fresh rosemary, finely chopped

¼ cup maple syrup

2 teaspoons cornstarch

1 tablespoon granular FruitSource (see Note, page 71)

Egg glaze

1 large egg yolk

1 teaspoon water

Position the rack in the bottom of the oven. Preheat the oven to 450°F. Butter a mixing bowl and a 14-inch round pizza pan.

Prepare the dough in the large bowl of an electric mixer fitted with the dough hook. Pour in the warm water, making sure it is not hotter than 115°F, and add the yeast. Let proof (active yeast will foam and smell yeasty) for 5 minutes. Add the milk and honey, and mix briefly on low speed. With the machine off, add the butter, flour, and salt. Turn on the machine and gradually increase the speed to high. Knead the dough until smooth, about 5 minutes. If kneading the dough by hand, knead for about 10 minutes.

Form into a ball and place in a buttered bowl. Cover with plastic wrap. Let rise until double in bulk, about 30 minutes.

Sprinkle the pizza pan with cornmeal, gently tapping the pan to shake off any excess.

While the dough is rising, prepare the topping. Melt 2 tablespoons of butter in a medium frying pan. Working with half of the apples at a time, slice them into ¼-inch-wide wedges and drop them into the pan. Cook the apples over medium-high heat until they begin to become tender and turn color, about 4 minutes. Gently turn them over to cook the other side. Transfer the cooked apples to a bowl and repeat with the remaining fruit. When the second batch of apples is cooked, transfer to the bowl. Reduce the heat, add the rosemary to the frying pan, and stir, cooking for 30 seconds. Add to the cooked apples. Toss the apple mixture with the maple syrup and cornstarch.

When the dough has risen, punch it down. On a lightly floured work surface, roll out the dough to fit the pizza pan and transfer it to the pan. Leaving a 1-inch-wide border, position the apples very close together on the dough to form concentric circles. Pour the juice from the pan over the apples. Sprinkle the FruitSource over the apples.

In a small bowl, mix the egg yolk with the water. Brush the border of the dough with the egg glaze.

Place the pizza on the bottom rack in the oven and reduce the heat to 375°F. Bake for about 25 minutes or until the crust is golden brown and the center has risen. Immediately transfer to a wire rack to cool.

Banana Chocolate Crêpes

Makes 4 servings

These chocolate crêpes are paired with sweet bananas heated in a rich barley malt caramel sauce and finished with a dark chocolate sauce and barley malt ice cream. Be sure to use bananas that are ripe, but that have not turned brown.

Caramel sauce

½ cup (1 stick) unsalted butter

½ cup barley malt syrup

¼ cup heavy cream

To serve

8 Chocolate Crêpes (page 213)

4 ripe bananas

1 recipe Dark Chocolate Sauce (page 218)

2 cups Malt Ice Cream (page 139)

For the caramel sauce, combine the butter and barley malt syrup in a small saucepan and bring to a boil, stirring until smooth. Stir in the heavy cream and cook a few moments longer. Set aside.

Line one large serving plate with parchment paper. Place 1 teaspoon of the caramel sauce in a large frying pan on low heat. When the sauce begins to melt, place a crêpe in the pan. As the crêpe warms, spoon a little caramel sauce over the top. When the underside is hot, about 1 minute, flip the crêpe over and cook for about 30 seconds. Working quickly with tongs, fold the crêpe in half and then into quarters and place on the parchment-lined plate. Keep warm in a 150° oven while you heat the remaining crêpes.

In the same frying pan on medium heat, add about 2 tablespoons of the caramel sauce. Slice each banana on a diagonal into about 6 pieces and place in the frying pan with the sauce and cook until the bottoms of the slices begin to caramelize, about 2 minutes. Gently turn the bananas over and cook about 1 minute, making sure the banana doesn't overcook, in which case the fruit will fall apart. Remove from the heat.

Place 2 crêpes on a warm dessert plate and drizzle some caramel sauce and chocolate sauce over the plate and the crêpes. Distribute the banana slices equally among the plates. Place a scoop of Malt Ice Cream on each plate and serve immediately.

Clarified Butter

There is no substitute for the flavor of butter, but the milk solids in butter cause it to burn when frying. Sometimes this is a desirable flavor, like in the Blueberry Cheese Blintzes recipe (page 14). When it is not, removing the milk solids will clarify the butter so it may be used for frying, much like oil. This is achieved by melting the butter over low heat and skimming off the foam that rises to the top. When it stops foaming you will be left with a clear yellow liquid on top and a white residue that sinks to the bottom. The clear yellow liquid is the clarified butter. Drain this into a bowl and discard the white residue. The clarified butter will keep for months in the refrigerator or freezer.

Cream Puffs

Makes 12 cream puffs

There is no limit to the flavors you can use to fill puff shells. I prefer mine with a mixture of pastry cream lightened with whipped cream. Sometimes I add sliced bananas, and other times I fill them with ice cream. Warmed Dark Chocolate Sauce (page 218) makes for a classic finish, while any fruit or caramel sauce will do equally as well.

1 cup heavy cream
1 recipe Pastry Cream (page 228)
12 large puff shells (see Pâte à Choux recipe, page 229)
1 recipe Dark Chocolate Sauce (page 218)

In a chilled, medium nonreactive bowl, whip the heavy cream until stiff. Fold it into the prepared pastry cream. Transfer the cream mixture to a pastry bag fitted with a plain tip. Make a whole in each puff large enough to insert the tip of the pastry bag. Pipe the cream into the puffs. To keep the shells crisp, fill them with the cream just before serving. To serve, spoon warm chocolate sauce over the top of each puff.

Date Nut Steamed Pudding

Makes one 6-cup mold; 10 servings

Because there is no baking, I like to toast the walnuts to bring out their flavor. Serve with whipped cream (see page 68).

8 ounces (½ pound) pitted dates, chopped

1 cup water

1 teaspoon baking soda

½ cup (1 stick) unsalted butter, at room temperature

1 cup maple sugar

3 large eggs

2 teaspoons pure vanilla extract

2 cups unbleached all-purpose flour

Pinch of salt

1 cup toasted walnuts, chopped

Butter the inside of a 2-quart pudding mold with a lid. Have ready a covered pot large enough to hold the pudding mold with at least a 2-inch clearance all around.

In a medium nonreactive bowl, mix together dates, water, and baking soda and let sit 3 hours or overnight at room temperature.

With an electric mixer on medium-high speed, cream together the butter and maple sugar until light and fluffy. Beat in the eggs one at a time. Mix in the date mixture and vanilla extract.

With the mixer on low speed, beat the flour and salt into the creamed butter mixture. Fold in the walnuts. Spoon the batter into the mold and cover the mold with the lid. Put the mold into the pot.

Fill the pot with enough hot water to reach one-third of the way up the sides of the mold. Cover the pot and bring the water to a boil. Immediately reduce the heat and keep the water at just a simmer. If the water boils, add cold water to control the temperature. The pudding needs to steam for about 1½ to 2 hours. When the pudding is done, a cake tester inserted into the center should come out clean. Cool the pudding completely before unmolding. Serve warm.

Fruit Soup

Makes about 6 cups; 6 servings

This soup may be served as a dessert or a first course for a summer meal. If you are able to buy cut pieces of melon, choose the ones which are fragrant and sweet smelling. I have used liquid FruitSource, but any liquid sweetener may be substituted. If you can't find it at your supermarket, cilantro may be found in Asian or South American markets. It is also referred to as fresh coriander or Chinese parsley.

1½ cups fresh orange juice
1½ cups tomato juice
2 cups sliced strawberries
1 cup seeded and cut watermelon (into chunks)
1 cup seeded and cut cantaloupe (into chunks)
1 large ripe firm mango
Pinch of salt
2 teaspoons liquid FruitSource (see Note, page 71), to taste
1 teaspoon lime zest, finely chopped
2 tablespoons chopped cilantro

Chill 6 dessert bowls.

In a large bowl, combine the orange juice, tomato juice, strawberries, watermelon, cantaloupe, and half of the mango. Purée the fruit mixture in a blender or food processor. Add the salt and taste for sweetness. Add the FruitSource to adjust the sweetness and add the lime zest. Chill for 1 hour. Just before serving, dice the remaining half of the mango and distribute it among the bowls. Stir the cilantro into the fruit purée and ladle into the bowls. Serve immediately.

Lemon Rice Cakes

Makes 6 servings

These cakes can be served in individual ramekins or baked in muffin tins for an on-the-go snack. They are also good accompanied by a fruit sauce.

1 cup Italian Arborio rice
2 cups whole milk
¼ cup maple syrup
1 teaspoon lemon zest, finely chopped
Pinch of ground cinnamon
½ cup (1 stick) unsalted butter
4 large egg yolks
¼ teaspoon salt
¼ cup organic Thompson dark raisins
1 large egg white, at room temperature

In a large heavy-bottomed saucepan, bring 4 cups of water to a boil. Add the rice, cook for 5 minutes, and drain. In a heavy saucepan, combine the milk and maple syrup and bring to a boil. Add the rice, lemon zest, and cinnamon. Reduce the heat to medium and stir constantly, cooking until all of the milk has been absorbed, about 30 minutes. Remove from the heat and add the butter.

In a medium bowl, beat the egg yolks. To temper the yolks, beat in a little of the warm rice mixture. While mixing the rice, slowly pour in the tempered yolks. Add the salt and raisins. Cool completely.

Preheat the oven to 400°F. Butter six ⅔-cup ramekins or a large muffin tin.

When the rice mixture has cooled, beat the egg white until firm, but not dry, in a clean, medium nonreactive bowl. Fold the egg white into the rice mixture. Spoon the rice mixture into the prepared cups. Bake for 10 minutes. Reduce the temperature to 350°F and continue baking until the centers have risen and a cake tester inserted in the center comes out clean, about 15 minutes. Let cool slightly. Serve warm or at room temperature.

Lime Trifle

Makes 8 servings

I suspect that no two trifles are ever the same, since these are a way to utilize ingredients on hand. Even though a specific flavored trifle requires some pre-planning, it gets assembled the day it is to be served. You can prepare the genoise in advance and keep it frozen until you need it. The lime curd and blueberry sauce can be made the day before.

Imbibing syrup

3 tablespoons honey

⅓ cup hot water

⅓ cup cold water

3 tablespoons fresh lime juice

Trifle

1 batch Genoise (page 222), let the cakes dry out

1 batch Lime Curd (page 223)

1 batch Blueberry Sauce (page 212)

¾ cup heavy cream

Have ready eight 8-ounce custard cups.

To prepare the imbibing syrup for this recipe, dissolve the honey in the hot water in a small bowl. Mix in the cold water and lime juice.

Use one of the custard cups like a cookie cutter to cut the genoise into 8 circles. Slice the circles to create two even layers. Working in an assembly line fashion, place a spoonful of the lime curd in the bottom of each custard cup. Top the custard with a layer of the genoise. Brush each layer with the imbibing syrup. Repeat, finishing with the imbibing syrup. Spoon about 2 tablespoons of the blueberry sauce over the top layer of the genoise and reserve any extra sauce for serving with the trifle.

Cover each cup with plastic wrap and chill for at least 3 hours or overnight. Prior to serving, whip the heavy cream into soft peaks in a medium bowl (see box, page 68). Place a dollop of whipped cream on the center of each trifle and serve immediately.

Note: Imbibing syrup is a sweet liqueur- or fruit-flavored syrup which is sprinkled lightly on cakes to add additional flavor and moisture.

Lokshen Kugel (Noodle Pudding)

Makes one 9 × 13-inch pudding; 15 servings

Sonny (my mother) does it again. Lokshen Kugel *means noodle pudding, a traditional Jewish dish that can be prepared either sweet or savory. In our home it was always sweet.*

1 pound broad egg noodles
½ cup (1 stick) unsalted butter
6 large eggs
½ cup orange juice concentrate, undiluted
½ cup maple syrup
1 cup unsweetened apple sauce
1 teaspoon pure vanilla extract
½ teaspoon salt
1 teaspoon ground cinnamon
1 cup golden raisins

In a very large saucepan, cook the noodles until tender in salted water according to the directions on the package. Drain and rinse. Return them to the pot and add the butter. Stir to melt.

Preheat the oven to 350°F. Butter one 9 × 13-inch baking dish.

In a bowl, beat all of the remaining ingredients together and pour into the noodles. With a wooden spoon, gently mix the noodles with the liquid ingredients. Pour into the prepared dish. Bake for 45 minutes to 1 hour, or until the corners are brown and a knife inserted into the center comes out clean. Let cool. To let the flavors blend, cover with plastic wrap and refrigerate overnight. Slice into 15 squares. Serve chilled or at room temperature.

Melon Soup

Makes about 6 cups, 8 servings

Fruit soups may be served either as a first course or a dessert. Use only sweet, ripe, juicy fruit. The quick preparation is disguised by the artistic presentation. Yogurt complements the fruits and serves as a garnish, but don't resist the desire to add some berries for contrast.

Soup

    1 large ripe cantaloupe (about 2½ pounds), peeled and seeded
    Pinch of salt
    2 teaspoons fresh lime juice
    ¼ cup vodka (optional)
    1 large honeydew (about 2 pounds), peeled and seeded

Garnish

    ⅔ cup plain yogurt
    1 teaspoon honey

Chill individual soup bowls—shallow bowls work best.

In a blender or food processor fitted with the steel blade, purée the cantaloupe. Add a pinch of salt and a few drops of lime juice. The cantaloupe should need only a little lime to bring out its flavor; only add more if needed. Add all of the vodka to this mixture. Refrigerate until chilled.

In a clean blender or food processor, repeat with the honeydew melon. Adjust the flavor with the salt and lime juice, keeping in mind the honeydew may require quite a bit more lime juice. Refrigerate until chilled.

For the garnish, in a small nonreactive bowl, mix together the yogurt and the honey until smooth.

To create a great presentation, the melon purées need to be poured into the bowl at the same time. This can be achieved by using two coffee cups. Fill 1 cup with some of the cantaloupe purée and the other with the honeydew purée. Holding 1 cup in each hand, pour the purées into

the bowl. They should meet in the middle, creating 2 half circles of color. Repeat with the other bowls.

For more decoration, draw a knife from the honeydew side into the cantaloupe purée. Continue until the desired marbling affect is complete. Finish each bowl by garnishing with a tablespoon of the yogurt. Serve immediately.

Peanuts and Popcorn

Makes about 10 cups

Growing up with Cracker Jacks™, one never really thinks about making caramel corn from scratch, but it's a great way to ensure freshness and to control the type of sweetener used. I like to add barley malt to give the caramel more depth in flavor. You'll have to supply the prizes!

¾ cup maple syrup
¼ cup honey
2 teaspoons barley malt syrup
⅓ cup unsalted butter
½ teaspoon baking soda
1 tablespoon pure vanilla extract
10 cups popped popcorn (use about ½ cup popcorn kernels)
½ cup roasted, unsalted peanuts

Preheat the oven to 350°F. Butter or line a baking sheet with parchment paper.

In a heavy, medium nonreactive saucepan, combine the maple syrup, honey, barley malt syrup, and butter. Bring to a boil and cook for 3 minutes. Remove from the heat and stir in the baking soda and vanilla extract. Place the popcorn and peanuts in a large bowl and coat them with the maple syrup mixture.

Transfer the popcorn mixture to the baking sheet. Bake for about 15 minutes or until the caramel turns a deep color, turning the popcorn every few minutes. Let cool. Store in an airtight container.

Orange Polenta Pudding with Black Raspberry Coulis

Makes 6 servings

The first time I made polenta, it ended up in a lumpy mess, but with some patience that has never to me happened again. Here, the creamy cornmeal is flavored with a honey-orange syrup, which calls for a whole orange including the skin. Therefore, I strongly recommend using organically grown fruit.

The pudding may be made in one large dish or individual custard cups. Even though black raspberries are native to North America, I see them at farmers' markets for only about one week each summer. If they are unavailable in your area, substitute the European native, the red raspberries.

Polenta

    1 seedless orange (organic), unpeeled
    1 tablespoon water
    ⅓ cup honey
    1 tablespoon Sucanat
    ½ teaspoon ground cinnamon
    ¼ teaspoon freshly grated nutmeg
    4½ cups whole milk
    ⅔ cup organic cornmeal
    3 tablespoons unsalted butter
    2 large eggs, lightly beaten

Black Raspberry Coulis

    2 cups black raspberries
    2 tablespoons maple syrup or honey
    ⅛ teaspoon ground cinnamon

Preheat the oven to 325°F. Butter one 8-inch-round glass baking dish. Have ready a pan large enough for the baking dish to create a bain-marie (see box, page 24).

Remove the stem and cut the orange into chunks. Place it in a food processor fitted with the steel blade. Add 1 tablespoon of water and about 1 tablespoon of the honey. Process until the orange is chopped into fine pieces. Transfer it to a small nonreactive saucepan and add the remaining honey and the Sucanat. Over medium-high heat, bring the mixture to a boil and continue boiling until the mixture is syrupy, about 8 minutes. Remove from the stove and stir in the cinnamon and nutmeg. Set aside.

In a separate saucepan, heat the milk over medium heat until it boils. Stirring constantly, very slowly add the cornmeal in small sprinkles. Reduce the heat to low and continue stirring until the cornmeal becomes thick and creamy. Remove from the stove and stir in the butter and eggs. Stir in the orange syrup. Transfer the polenta to the baking dish. Set the baking dish into the pan and fill the pan with enough hot water to reach half way up the sides of the dish. Bake until a knife inserted into the center comes out clean, about 1 hour and 15 minutes.

To prepare the coulis, in a nonreactive saucepan, combine 1½ cups of the berries with the sweetener. Reserve the remaining berries for garnishing the servings. Bring syrup mixture to a soft boil over medium heat. Gently cook the berries until they are plump and juice extracts, about 5 minutes. Stir in the cinnamon. To remove the seeds, press the berry mixture through a fine-meshed sieve set over a bowl. Refrigerate until chilled. Serve the pudding warm or at room temperature with the coulis and the reserved berries.

Panettone Bread Pudding

Makes 12 servings

I know that most people do not usually have a naturally sweetened panettone hanging around, much less a stale one. But if you make the Panettone recipe on page 34, you could save one of the loaves for a later date. Otherwise, any rich bread like challah or brioche can be used.

Panettone

   1 Panettone (page 34)

Custard

   8 large eggs
   4 cups half and half
   ½ cup honey
   1 tablespoon pure vanilla extract
   Pinch of salt

To serve

   1 batch *Crème Anglaise* (page 215)

Butter one 3-quart baking dish. Have ready a pan large enough for the baking dish to create a bain-marie (see box, page 24).

Cut the panettone into ½-inch-thick slices. Layer them in the baking dish by overlapping the pieces to fit the shape of the dish.

In a large bowl, beat together the eggs, cream, honey, vanilla, and salt until thoroughly blended. Pour the custard over the panettone. To enable the panettone to absorb the custard, cover the baking dish with aluminum foil and place a plate on top of the foil. Place some heavy object on the plate, and let sit for at least 1 hour.

Preheat the oven to 325°F. Remove the weight and set the bread pudding dish in the other pan. Pour hot water into the larger pan to come half way up the sides of the pudding dish. Bake for about 1½ hours or until the center rises and the top browns. The pudding may look done long before the baking time has past because the top will brown, but make sure the center rises to ensure the custard is cooked throughout. Serve warm with the *crème anglaise*.

Sautéed Figs with Pine Nuts

Makes 4 servings

If you have never experienced fresh figs, this is a good way to start!

2 tablespoons unsalted butter
2 tablespoons honey
12 ripe fresh figs, cut in half lengthwise
½ cup Marsala wine
2 tablespoons toasted pine nuts
½ cup mascarpone cheese (optional, at room temperature)

In a heavy frying pan, melt the butter over medium heat. Add the honey and the figs, cut side down. Cook for 3 minutes. Add the wine and bring to a boil. Continue cooking, basting the fruit with the liquid, until the liquid is reduced by half, about 5 minutes. Transfer to a serving dish. Sprinkle with the pine nuts. Serve with a dollop of mascarpone cheese, if desired (see page 50).

Pecan Caramel Banana Fritters

Makes 4 servings

One secret to good fritters is a batter that will cling to the fruit. Here, the cling is taken two steps further for a sweet indulgence. Ripe bananas are coated in a light batter, deep fried, then dipped in caramel and rolled in chopped pecans. Other helpful things are additional hands in the kitchen and a supply of bamboo skewers.

Batter

1 large egg yolk

⅓ cup milk

2 teaspoons honey

1 teaspoon unsalted butter, melted

½ cup unbleached all-purpose flour

¼ teaspoon salt

¼ teaspoon freshly grated nutmeg

About 1 quart vegetable oil for deep frying

1 large egg white, at room temperature

Sauce

¼ cup unsalted butter

⅓ cup maple syrup

⅓ cup barley malt syrup

1 teaspoon pure vanilla extract

1 tablespoon fresh orange juice

Fruit

4 ripe, firm medium bananas

Garnish

⅔ cup pecans, finely chopped

In a small bowl, mix together the egg yolk, milk, honey, butter, flour, salt, and nutmeg until smooth. Cover with plastic wrap and let rest for at least 2 hours.

Meanwhile, prepare the caramel sauce. In a small, heavy saucepan combine the butter and the maple and barley malt syrups. Bring the mixture to a boil, stirring to combine. Let boil for about 1 minute. Remove from the heat and stir in the vanilla extract and orange juice. Warm the sauce just before you begin to fry the fritters. Have ready the nuts in a small bowl.

Either in a deep fryer or a deep, heavy saucepan, heat the oil to a constant 375°F on a frying thermometer. Or test by dropping about 1 teaspoon of batter into the oil, which should immediately sizzle around the batter. (If the oil begins to smoke, it is too hot, and you should lower the heat.)

In a small bowl, beat the egg white until firm, but not dry. Fold into the batter.

To prevent discoloration, work with one banana at a time. Cut the banana into 1-inch chunks. When the oil has reached the proper temperature, place the banana chunk on a bamboo skewer and into the batter, maneuvering with the skewer to shake off any excess batter. Gently drop the coated chunk into the hot oil. Without crowding the pot, add additional chunks. Cook until golden brown, about 1 minute, turning as the underside browns. Use tongs to remove from the oil and pat gently on paper towel to eliminate any excess oil. Let rest on a wire rack set over paper towel to catch any excess oil.

While the second batch of fritters are frying, use a skewer to dip the cooked fritters in the warm caramel sauce. Shake off any excess sauce and roll the fritters in the chopped nuts. Transfer to a serving dish. Work quickly to finish all the fritters. Serve immediately.

Pumpkin Steamed Pudding

Makes one 6-cup mold; 10 servings

Before I had formally written this recipe, I received a call from my sister-in-law, Patricia. My 10-year-old niece, Helen, loved the sample I sent them so much, she was afraid she was going to have to wait for the book to be published before she could get a copy of the recipe. Patricia assured her there was a faster way—the telephone!

Pudding

¾ cup (1½ sticks) unsalted butter, at room temperature

2 cups maple sugar

3 large eggs

1½ cups pumpkin purée, fresh or canned

2¼ cups unbleached all-purpose flour

2¼ teaspoons baking powder

½ teaspoon ground ginger

¾ teaspoon salt

1 teaspoon ground cinnamon

¼ teaspoon ground cardamom

¼ teaspoon ground allspice

⅛ teaspoon freshly ground black pepper

To serve

1 batch *Crème Anglaise,* orange flavored
(see recipe and Note, page 215)

Butter the inside of one 2-quart pudding mold with a lid. Have ready a covered pot large enough to hold the pudding mold with at least a 2-inch clearance all around.

With an electric mixer, cream together the butter and maple sugar until light and fluffy. Beat in the eggs one at a time. Add the pumpkin purée.

In the large bowl of an electric mixer, sift together the flour, baking powder, ginger, salt, cinnamon, cardamom, allspice, and black pepper. With the mixer on low speed, beat the dried ingredients into the pumpkin mixture. Spoon the batter into the mold and cover the mold with the lid. Put the mold into the pot.

Fill the pot with enough hot water to reach one-third of the way up the sides of the mold. Cover the pot and bring the water to a boil. Immediately reduce the heat to medium low and keep the water at just a simmer. If the water boils, add cold water to control the temperature. The pudding needs to steam for 1½ to 2 hours. When the pudding is done, a skewer inserted into the center should come out clean. Cool the pudding completely before unmolding. Serve the pudding warm with orange-flavored *crème anglaise*.

Tiramisu

Makes 6 servings

The name says it all—"pick me up." This dessert has taken North America by storm. It's Italy's version of trifle. I have used my genoise cake to replace the traditional lady fingers. The cake must be baked in advance so it has time to become stale. In addition, the dessert must be assembled at least 6 hours before serving. Depending on the type of occasion, the choice of presentation is up to you. I like to make this in a decorative bowl. It may also be made in a loaf pan, sliced and served individually. In either case, the container needs to hold 6 cups. Buon appetito!

1 batch Genoise (page 222)
2 large egg yolks
2 tablespoons maple syrup
1 cup mascarpone cheese, at room temperature (see box, page 50)
1 cup heavy cream
½ teaspoon pure vanilla extract
¼ cup brewed espresso, at room temperature
¼ cup sweet Marsala wine
Unsweetened cocoa powder for dusting
Finely ground espresso beans for dusting

Prepare the genoise according to the directions on page 222 and allow it to become stale. (Leave it uncovered at room temperature for at least 1 day.)

In a medium-large bowl set over simmering water, beat the egg yolks and maple syrup with an electric mixer until the mixture is warm to the touch and is pale yellow, about 5 minutes. Remove the bowl from the heat and continue beating on high speed until the mixture has cooled and its consistency has become thick and ribbony, and it has tripled in volume, about 5 minutes. Beat in the mascarpone until smooth. Be careful not to overbeat or the mixture will appear to curdle.

In a chilled, medium bowl, whip the heavy cream with the vanilla extract until soft peaks form. Fold the whipped cream into the mascarpone mixture. In a small bowl, mix together the brewed espresso and the Marsala wine.

To assemble, slice or tear the genoise to create one layer in the dish. Sprinkle the layer lightly with some of the Marsala mixture. Dust lightly with some cocoa powder and espresso grounds. Spread one-third of the cream over the cake. Repeat to form 2 more layers ending with a layer of cream. Chill for at least 6 hours. Just before serving, sprinkle the top liberally with cocoa powder.

Chapter Nine

FOUNDATIONS AND FINISHING TOUCHES

*E*very baker needs a collection of recipes for basic components that will form the foundation for infinite possibilities. Most dessert cookbooks include their own version of these types of recipes, but since these recipes are free of refined sugar, it was essential to provide a selection of naturally sweetened alternatives.

There are endless variations to these basic recipes. By making even the most minor alterations, like adding a pinch of spice or choosing a different flavor of liqueur, a new creation comes into being. If you choose not to waver from the original recipe, you can still produce classic combinations that are sure never to disappoint.

In this chapter you will find all the usual basics like pastry creams, buttercreams, and sauces. If you have already mastered any of these components using white sugar, you may be surprised to learn that using natural sugars requires the same techniques. If you are making these basics for the fist time, you will be learning to master classic techniques that are invaluable. In either case, this chapter will provide you with the components you need to make professionally finished, fantastic-tasting desserts.

Apricot Pastry Cream

Makes about 3 cups

The addition of apricots makes for a rich yet refreshing cream. Try using this cream for a trifle or as a filling for plain genoise cake. It is also great with fresh figs.

1 cup dried apricots
1 recipe Pastry Cream (page 228)
½ teaspoon pure vanilla extract
⅔ cup heavy cream

In a small saucepan, place apricots and add enough water to cover. Cook over low heat until the apricots are soft and plump, 20 to 30 minutes. In the work bowl of a food processor fitted with a steel blade, purée the apricots until smooth. Allow to cool. Fold the apricots into the prepared pastry cream.

In a chilled, medium bowl, add the vanilla extract to the heavy cream and whip until firm. Stir one-third of the whipped cream into the apricot pastry cream to loosen, and fold in the remaining whipped cream.

Blueberry Sauce

Makes about 2 cups

This sauce is so versatile you can eat it all day long—at breakfast with pancakes, at lunch over ice cream, or after dinner with trifle.

2 cups fresh blueberries, rinsed and stemmed
⅔ cup apple juice, not from concentrate
½ teaspoon ground cinnamon
3 to 4 tablespoons maple syrup or honey
1½ teaspoons cornstarch
About 1 tablespoon cold water
1 teaspoon orange zest, finely chopped
1 tablespoon orange liqueur
1 tablespoon unsalted butter (optional)

In a medium nonreactive saucepan, combine the blueberries, apple juice, and cinnamon. Cook over medium heat and bring to a gentle boil. Cook until the fruit is heated through and the mixture begins to be colored from the berries, about 5 minutes. Taste for sweetness and add the sweetener to adjust.

In a small bowl, blend the cornstarch in about 1 tablespoon cold water until smooth. Pour the cornstarch paste into the fruit mixture, stirring constantly, and bring to a boil for 30 seconds. Remove from the heat and stir in the orange zest and orange liqueur. Add the butter, if desired. Serve warm or chilled.

Chocolate Crêpes

Makes twelve 8-inch crêpes

3 large eggs
⅔ cup milk
⅔ cup water
¼ teaspoon salt
1 tablespoon honey
2 tablespoons peanut oil, plus more oil for frying
1 cup unbleached all-purpose flour
2 tablespoons unsweetened cocoa powder

Combine all of the ingredients in a blender or the work bowl of a food processor fitted with the steel blade, and blend for 30 seconds. Let the batter rest for at least 2 hours before frying. It may be refrigerated overnight.

To fry the crêpes, use an 8-inch round bottom cast-iron skillet or a nonstick frying pan with an 8-inch-round bottom surface. To prevent the crêpes from sticking to the pan, lightly oil the pan by dipping a paper towel into some cooking oil and then wiping the surface of the pan with the towel. Heat the pan over medium-high heat until drops of water sizzle when sprinkled into the pan.

Using a ladle, pour some batter onto the surface of the pan and swirl to spread the batter. Shake out any excess batter that does not immediately adhere. Cook until the bottom of the crêpe becomes browned and the top is dry, about 1 minute. Flip the crêpe over and cook until the second side is also lightly browned, about 45 seconds. Turn the crêpe out of the pan onto a plate. Place a square of waxed paper onto the crêpe. Return the pan to the heat, lightly oil the pan, and repeat. Adjust the temperature as necessary, making sure the pan remains hot, but not so hot that the crêpe burns before it cooks. After they cool, the crêpes may be wrapped and frozen. Let them come to room temperature before using.

Chocolate Pastry

Makes dough for one 10-inch round tart

This is a bittersweet chocolate pastry that adds another flavor and aesthetic dimension to your dessert. Try it with the Banana Cream filling (page 154) or your favorite pastry cream.

1 cup unbleached all-purpose flour
½ cup unsweetened cocoa powder
½ cup maple sugar
Pinch of salt
1 large egg
1 large egg yolk
½ cup (1 stick) unsalted butter, at room temperature

In a large bowl, sift together the flour, cocoa, maple sugar, and salt. Either with a wooden spoon or by hand, mix in the egg and egg yolk until the mixture looks crumbly. Add the butter and blend until you have a smooth dough. Wrap in plastic and chill for at least one hour.

Preheat the oven to 350°F.

On a lightly floured work surface, roll out the dough to ⅛-inch thick. If the dough becomes soft and sticky, dust with more flour. When the dough has been rolled to the desired size, brush off any excess flour.

Transfer the pastry to a 10-inch-round tart pan with a removable bottom. Use your hands to repair any tears in the dough and trim the sides. Pierce the bottom with the tines of a fork and freeze for 10 minutes. Bake for about 20 minutes, watching carefully to make sure the crust doesn't burn. The crust is done when it is firm and comes away from the sides. Let cool before filling.

Crème Anglaise (Custard Sauce)

Makes about 2 cups

This is a classic custard sauce that may be served warm or chilled. Egg yolks and patience are the thickening agents.

6 large egg yolks
⅓ cup honey or maple syrup
1½ cups warm milk
1 tablespoon pure vanilla extract
3 tablespoons unsalted butter (optional)
2 tablespoons rum or other liqueur (optional)
1 teaspoon orange zest, finally chopped (optional)

In a medium saucepan, use a whisk to beat the yolks and sweetener until the mixture is pale yellow, about 3 minutes. Using a wooden spoon, stir the egg mixture while gradually adding the warm milk.

Heat the mixture over medium-low heat. To create the least amount of foam possible, use the spoon to constantly stir the mixture. Be sure to reach the entire bottom and sides of the pan. If the mixture gets too hot, it will scramble the eggs. It is important to circulate the liquid to prevent the bottom from overcooking before the rest of the liquid has been heated. Toward the final stages, if you are having some difficulty controlling the heat, remove the pan completely from the stove, stir, and return to the heat. Repeat as necessary.

The mixture is done when it is thick enough to lightly coat the spoon and holds when your finger is drawn through it. Pass through a strainer set over a clean bowl. Add the vanilla extract and any of the flavorings, if desired.

Serve warm or chilled. The sauce may be made in advance and stored in an airtight container refrigerated for 4 days. To rewarm, place the sauce in the top of a double boiler and cook over gently simmering water until warm to the touch, about 4 minutes, stirring occasionally.

Note: The Crème Anglaise can be flavored with orange zest a nice, fresh taste; use about 1 teaspoon of finely grated zest.

Crêpes

Makes about fourteen 8-inch crêpes

In North America, we have hot dog stands; in Paris, they have crêpe stands. And like a certain hot dog stand here at home, there is always one crêpe stand that stands out! My brother found that special crêpe stand where the owner was an "artist." Other stands had the crêpes already prepared waiting to be purchased, but not at this stand. Here, they were made to order. As I watched the artist at work, the secret to the crêpes was revealed. He used a device similar to a squeegee across the surface to close any holes and remove any excess batter. Once I saw this technique, I no longer worried about not getting the perfect amount of batter right the first time. I swirl the pan to cover any holes and shake off the excess batter. If it's been a while since my last crêpe creation, I admit it takes a few less-than-perfect ones before I get the rhythm back, but it always returns. One sure way to prevent this awkwardness is to make crêpes all the time.

3 large eggs
⅔ cup milk
⅔ cup water
¼ teaspoon salt
3 tablespoons peanut oil, plus more for frying
1 cup unbleached all-purpose flour

Combine all the ingredients in a blender or the work bowl of a food processor fitted with the steel blade, and blend for 30 seconds. Let the batter rest for at least 2 hours before frying. It may be refrigerated overnight.

Have ready a plate for the cooked crêpes and 4-inch-square pieces of waxed paper to place in between the crêpes as they are stacked.

To fry the crêpes, use a well-seasoned cast-iron skillet or a non-stick frying pan with an 8-inch-round bottom surface. To prevent the crêpes from sticking to the pan, lightly oil the pan by dipping a paper towel into some cooking oil and then wiping the surface of the pan with the towel. Heat the pan over medium-high heat until a few drops of water sizzle when sprinkled into the pan.

Using a ladle, pour some batter onto the surface of the pan and swirl to spread the batter over the entire surface. Shake out any excess batter that does not immediately adhere. Cook until the bottom of the crêpe becomes browned and the top is dry. Flip the crêpe over and cook until the second side is also lightly browned, about 45 seconds.

Turn the crêpe out of the pan onto the plate. Place a square of waxed paper onto the crêpe. Return the pan to the heat, lightly oil the pan, and repeat. Adjust the temperature as necessary making sure the pan remains hot, but not so hot that the crêpe burns before it cooks. The crêpes may be frozen. Let them come to room temperature before using.

Honey Lemon Cream Cheese Icing

Makes about 4 cups

The sweetness of this icing may be adjusted to suit your taste. When adding more honey, watch that the consistency remains spreadable. The icing will firm up when refrigerated, but if you add too much honey, it may become too soft or loose for the center of a double-layer cake.

1½ pounds firm cream cheese, at room temperature
1½ cups (3 sticks) unsalted butter
½ cup honey, or to taste
1 teaspoon pure vanilla extract
2 tablespoons freshly squeezed lemon juice (optional)
1 tablespoon lemon zest, finely chopped (optional)

In a medium bowl, using an electric mixer on low speed, cream together the cream cheese and butter. Add the honey to taste, making sure it does not become too soft. Stir in the vanilla extract, lemon juice, and zest, if desired. Spread on your choice of cake.

Dark Chocolate Sauce

Makes about 3 cups

Depending on your taste, this sauce can be made and enjoyed in two ways. It begins as a sauce with an intense, dark chocolate flavor. With the addition of heavy cream, it becomes even richer and smoother. Either way, no one will want to miss a drop.

1 cup semi-sweet grain-sweetened chocolate chips (see Note, page 101)
¾ cup (1½ sticks) unsalted butter
¾ cup maple sugar
¾ cup cocoa powder
¼ cup strong coffee, at room temperature
½ cup honey
Pinch of ground cinnamon
Pinch of salt
1 cup heavy cream (optional)

In a medium bowl set over simmering water, melt the chocolate and the butter. Stir until smooth.

In a medium saucepan, combine the maple sugar, cocoa powder, and coffee and cook over low heat until smooth. Stir in the butter mixture and the honey. Add the cinnamon and salt. At this point the sauce will be very dark with an intense flavor. Either remove from the heat, or for a richer sauce, stir in the heavy cream, continuing to cook until smooth.

Serve the sauce warm or at room temperature. Store it in an airtight container and refrigerate for up to 4 weeks without the heavy cream, or for 2 weeks with the cream.

Graham Cracker Crust

Makes one 10-inch-round crust

A company by the name of Hain makes many naturally sweetened products. See the Source List, page 235, for more information. Their Honey Grahams are delicious and can be used to make a great graham cracker crust.

15 graham crackers, such as Honey Grahams by Hain
½ teaspoon ground cinnamon (optional)
½ teaspoon vanilla extract
½ cup (1 stick) unsalted butter, melted

Preheat the oven to 350°F.

Crumbs may be made either by hand, placing the crackers in a plastic bag and crushing them with a rolling pin, or by machine, breaking the crackers into large pieces and whirring them into crumbs in the bowl of a food processor fitted with a steel blade. (Makes about 1½ cups of crumbs.)

To make the crust, transfer the crumbs to a mixing bowl. Add cinnamon. Add the vanilla extract to the butter and pour the butter mixture into the crumbs. Mix thoroughly. Place the crumb mixture into the pan. Use your hands to press the crumbs into an even layer. Bake for 5 minutes. Let the crust cool before filling.

French Buttercream

Makes about 4 cups

The difference between French and Italian buttercream is the eggs. The latter uses only egg whites; the former uses whole eggs and additional yolks. The yolks create a more stable buttercream that may be frozen and rewhipped. Cooking the sweetener produces a smooth, rich, and less sweet-tasting buttercream. Flavor the base with fruit purées and different liqueurs.

Buttercream

> 2 large eggs, at room temperature
> 2 large egg yolks, at room temperature
> 1 cup maple syrup
> 1¾ cups (3½ sticks) unsalted butter

Flavor ideas

> 1 tablespoon instant espresso dissolved in 1 tablespoon of water
> ¼ cup flavored liqueur, such as orange or cassis
> 1 to 2 tablespoons pure extract, such as vanilla or almond
> ⅓ cup fruit purée, such as strawberry
> ¼ cup finely ground toasted nuts
> ¾ cup semi-sweet grain-sweetened chocolate chips (see Note, page 101), melted and cooled

In a large bowl of an electric mixer, begin beating the eggs and yolks at a slow speed.

In a medium saucepan, bring the syrup to a boil over high heat. Continue boiling until the syrup reaches just past the soft ball stage, 242°F on a candy thermometer. Or test by placing a few drops of the syrup into cold water; the syrup should hold its shape and feel soft to the touch.

With the mixer on low, slowly pour the syrup into the beaten eggs. Gradually increase the speed of the mixer and continue beating until the egg mixture becomes cool, about 15 minutes.

In a small bowl, beat the butter until light and fluffy. With the mixer on medium, add the butter by tablespoons to the egg mixture (see Note).

Note: The mixture may appear to curdle, but [do] not worry. However, if [the] egg mixture deflates with the addition [of] the first few spoonfuls of butter, it is [too] warm; chill the mixture for about 30 minutes befor[e] proceeding. Once chilled, continue beat[ing] in the butter

Add the desired flavoring. Increase the speed to high and continue beating until light and fluffy.

For best results, use the buttercream immediately, but leftover buttercream may be refrigerated for 5 days. Bring it to room temperature and beat with an electric mixer until light and fluffy. Frozen buttercream should be defrosted in the refrigerator before rewhipping. It will keep frozen for about 1 month.

Hazelnut Frangipane

Makes about 2 cups

Frangipane is a light, buttery nut-cake batter that may be used in two ways: First as a baked filling for pastry that is then topped with custard or fruit, and second, in pastry as a base for fruit that will cook together, allowing the frangipane to absorb the fruit juices. It may be made with different types of nuts such as almonds, pecans, or walnuts. Depending on the nuts, the flavorings may also vary.

⅔ cup skinless hazelnuts (see box, page 83)
½ cup maple sugar
¼ cup (½ stick) unsalted butter, at room temperature
2 large eggs
¼ cup unbleached all-purpose flour
1 teaspoon pure vanilla extract
1 teaspoon lemon zest, finely chopped

In the bowl of a food processor fitted with the steel blade, combine the hazelnuts and maple sugar and pulse until the nuts are finely ground. Transfer the nut mixture to a bowl and whisk in the butter. Mix in the remaining ingredients until smooth. If the batter is runny, chill to firm it. Because of the raw egg, the mixture should be used within 3 to 4 days. Keep it refrigerated until ready to use in recipes.

Genoise

Makes two 9 × ¾-inch-round cakes

This all-purpose cake forms the foundation for infinite recipes. Although there are many variations on the amounts of egg and butter, this recipe has been developed to best suit the use of maple syrup. I have had the best success baking it in two pans, creating layers that are about ¾-inch thick. They can be split or left whole depending on their final use. If your recipe calls for only one cake, freeze the remainder for future use. The texture of this light sponge cake lends itself well to trifles and cakes brushed with imbibing syrups.

½ cup cake flour

¼ teaspoon baking powder

¼ cup cornstarch

Pinch of salt

3 large eggs

3 large egg yolks

⅔ cup maple syrup

Preheat the oven to 350°F. Butter two 9 × 1½-inch-round cake pans.

In a small bowl, mix together the flour, baking powder, cornstarch, and salt. Sift twice and set aside.

In a large heat-proof bowl, use an electric mixer to beat the eggs and yolks together until they begin to lighten. Add the maple syrup in a slow stream. Place the bowl over simmering water and whisk constantly until the egg mixture is warm, about 120°F on an instant-read thermometer. The mixture should increase in volume and hold ribbons. To test, a ribbon should be created when some of the mixture is lifted and dropped back into the bowl. If a ribbon forms and then dissipates slowly, it is ready. Remove from the heat and beat with an electric mixer on high speed until the egg mixture is cool to the touch, about 10 minutes.

Sift the flour mixture over the egg mixture, in 4 or 5 additions, folding in each addition with a large rubber spatula. Divide the batter evenly between the two pans and bake until the cake has risen and is firm to the touch, about 18 minutes. The cake will fall, but remain light in texture. Loosen the sides of the cakes and invert the pans to transfer the cakes to a wire rack. Reinvert onto another rack and let cool.

Lime Curd

Makes about 3 cups

To add a twist to your desserts, substitute this recipe for lemon curd.

6 large eggs
2 large egg yolks
1 scant cup of maple syrup
⅔ cup freshly squeezed lime juice
½ cup (1 stick) unsalted butter, cut into ½-inch chunks
1 tablespoon lime zest, finely chopped

In a stainless steel bowl, use a whisk to combine the eggs, egg yolks, maple syrup, and lime juice. Add the butter and set the bowl over a pot of simmering water. Whisking constantly, cook the mixture until it becomes very thick, being careful not to let the mixture come to a boil. It should take about 8 minutes for it to thicken once it has become hot to the touch.

Immediately remove the bowl from the simmering water and pass the mixture through a strainer set over a clean bowl. Stir in the lime zest. To prevent a skin from forming on the curd, cover the mixture with plastic wrap pressed to the surface. Let cool.

Italian Meringue Chocolate Buttercream

Makes about 4 cups

The first time I attempted to make this type of buttercream, I was very overwhelmed by having to simultaneously attend to the egg whites and the syrup. Once I realized I could slow down the machine, if not turn it off completely, while I waited for the temperature of the syrup to rise, it also occurred to me that I was the one in control, not the ingredients!

With practice you will develop your own timing and come to realize classic recipes are usually more forgiving than you think. That could be why they have persevered long enough to become classics.

5 ounces unsweetened chocolate, melted

4 large egg whites, at room temperature

Pinch of salt

¼ teaspoon cream of tartar

1¼ cups maple syrup

¼ cup water

1 cup (2 sticks) unsalted butter, at room temperature

1 teaspoon pure vanilla extract

In a small, heat resistant bowl set over simmering water, melt the chocolate. Set aside and let it cool.

In the large bowl of an electric mixer, begin beating the egg whites at low speed until they are foamy. Add the salt and cream of tartar. Gradually increase the speed to medium-fast and continue beating the egg whites until stiff, shiny peaks are formed, making sure to not over beat the whites while the syrup is cooking.

Meanwhile, in a medium saucepan, bring the maple syrup and water to a boil over high heat. Continue boiling until the syrup reaches just past the soft ball stage, 242°F on a candy thermometer, or when it is dropped in cold water it forms a soft, but firm ball.

With the mixer speed on slow, dribble the syrup into the beaten egg whites. Gradually increase the speed of the mixer and continue beating until the egg whites become cool and form stiff, shiny and upstanding peaks, 15 to 20 minutes.

In a small bowl, beat the butter until light and fluffy. With the mixer on medium, add the butter by tablespoonfuls to the meringue (see Note).

Add the vanilla and chocolate. Increase the speed to high and continue beating until light and fluffy.

It is best to use immediately to frost cakes. The leftover buttercream may be refrigerated for five days. Bring to room temperature and beat with an electric mixer until light and fluffy.

Note: The meringue may appear to curdle; do not worry. If the butter looks like it is melting because the meringue is too warm, chill the mixture for about 30 minutes before proceeding. Once chilled, return to the heat.

Boiling Maple Syrup

Follow these tips for boiling maple syrup: Use a large saucepan, such as one 3-quart pan to boil 1 cup of syrup. The syrup boils quickly; adding a little water will give you more time and control. The syrup will foam up, filling the pan as its temperature increases. Use a candy thermometer to check for your desired temperature.

Pastry

Makes 1 double-crust 9-inch pie

I have a framed picture of Julia Child in my kitchen. People immediately ask if it is my mother. Perhaps, in another lifetime, is my usual reply.

This is the ultimate pastry recipe and it is all Julia's. I have been making it since 1978, when it was first published in her book, Julia Child and Company and I was fifteen. Over the years I must have read thousands of pastry recipes. Though trying only a few, I quickly discovered they were usually more trouble to make and produced inferior results.

During my restaurant baking experience, I have watched chef's eyes light up as they sampled my creations using this recipe. As a self-taught baker, I have always great pleasure when these same chefs have cautiously asked if I would reveal to them "my recipe." I always let them know my source.

In minutes, this recipe creates the closest thing to actual French pastry this side of the Atlantic. I use it for both sweet and savory tarts. Julia suggests sweetening the dough for desserts, but I have never found it necessary. It is so well formulated I have made it in batches that were literally ten times the basic measurements. The secret is to keep the butter, shortening, and water as cold as possible and not to overwork the dough.

This past Thanksgiving was spent dining on the amazing culinary creations of our friend Evelyn in New York. As I thankfully consumed her wonderful multi-course dinner, I sat in full view of the forthcoming desserts. As I tasted the first, a Shaker pie, my immediate thought was that for the first time I had found a pastry that tasted as delicious as mine. When I was able to stop eating long enough to compliment Evelyn on her treasure, I inquired about the source of her pastry recipe—Julia Child, of course.

1½ cups unbleached all-purpose flour
½ cup cake or pastry flour
Pinch of salt
6 ounces (1½ sticks) unsalted butter, chilled
2 tablespoons vegetable shortening, frozen
½ cup iced water

In the bowl of a food processor fitted with a steel blade, combine the flours and the salt. Process for a few seconds to mix the ingredients together.

Cut the butter into ½ inch chunks and distribute on top of the flour. Cut in the shortening. Using an on/off pulsing action, letting it run for half a second at a time, process 10 to 15 times. Check to see that the butter is breaking up into coarse pieces, the size of lentils. Do not overprocess.

With the water poised over the opening of the machine, pour in one-third of the water, and pulse 2 to 3 times. Add another third of the water and pulse again. The dough should just begin to mass together with some coarse, unformed bits. Touch the dough to feel if it is moister than it looks; if it seems too dry, add the remaining water and pulse 1 or 2 more times. Turn the dough onto a work surface and, using the heel of your hand, work it quickly and briefly to mass it together to form a cake. Wrap in plastic wrap and refrigerate it for at least 1 hour.

The dough can be refrigerated for up to 3 days before the unbleached flour will start to turn gray. The dough may be frozen for several months if wrapped in plastic wrap and placed in an airtight container. Let it defrost in the refrigerator before rolling out, or it may be rolled and set into the desired pan before freezing.

Pastry Cream

Makes about 1½ cups

There are many different ways to make pastry cream, which is a delicious staple for an infinite array of desserts. This is a versatile recipe that is easy to make and can be embellished with whipped cream or puréed fruits.

1 cup milk

1 large egg

2 tablespoons honey or maple syrup

1 tablespoon unbleached all-purpose flour

2 teaspoons cornstarch

2 tablespoons unsalted butter

1 teaspoon pure vanilla extract

1 teaspoon orange zest, finely chopped (optional)

In a medium saucepan, warm the milk. In a medium bowl, whisk together the egg and the honey. Add the flour and the cornstarch, beating until smooth. Gradually pour the warm milk into the egg mixture. Stir until blended.

Pour the mixture into a clean saucepan and cook over medium heat, stirring constantly. Let the mixture come to a boil. Cook for 1 minute. Remove from the heat and immediately pass the mixture through a strainer set over a clean bowl.

Stir in the butter and the vanilla extract, and add the zest, if desired. To prevent a skin from forming on the cream, cover it with plastic wrap pressed to the surface. Chill. The pastry cream will keep for about 4 days.

Pâte à Choux

Makes about 12 large puffs

Note: Adding the egg to the batter may be done by hand. With each addition, the egg will initially separate from the flour mixture making it difficult to mix, but it will become incorporated. The final batter should just hold its shape. If you are not sure, bake a test puff. Add more egg if necessary.

Ever since I can remember, for special occasions my mother would make pâte à choux. *If she wasn't serving them for dessert as cream puffs, she would make them into an hors d'oeurvre of miniature puffs stuffed with mushrooms and onions. My mother learned to make them from her aunt, who would fill them with ice cream.*

The consistency of the batter is very important. It should be smooth and shiny and just able to hold its shape. If your batter doesn't puff properly, beat in a little more egg and bake a test puff.

1 cup water
½ cup (1 stick) unsalted butter
Pinch of salt
1 cup unbleached all-purpose flour
5 large eggs, plus one additional egg slightly beaten

Preheat the oven to 425°F. Line a baking sheet with parchment paper.

In a small saucepan, combine the water, butter, and salt and bring the mixture to a rolling boil. Remove the pan from the heat and add the flour all at once. Quickly stir the mixture to incorporate the flour. Continue stirring and return the pan to the heat. Cook until the flour mixture forms a ball and pulls away from the sides of the pan. Remove from the stove and cool briefly.

Using a hand-held electric mixer, beat the eggs one at a time into the flour mixture. Each egg should be completely incorporated before the next addition (see Note).

Drop by spoonfuls or pipe into desired shapes, such as lines for éclairs, on the baking sheet. Bake for 20 minutes. Reduce the heat to 375°F and continue baking for about another 15 minutes. The puffs should be golden brown and feel crisp to the touch. To let the steam escape, as soon as they are done, remove them from the oven and quickly make a small slash in the side of each puff; bake for about 5 more minutes. Cool before filling.

Sour Cherry Sauce

Makes about 2 cups

Most people are familiar with jars of sour cherries from Hungary. Even my Hungarian friend, Amy, said she didn't know of anyone who still goes to the trouble of using fresh sour cherries for traditional recipes. But once Amy tasted this sauce, she was sorry they didn't.

2 cups pitted sour cherries

½ cup apple juice, not from concentrate

2 tablespoons maple syrup, to taste

⅛ teaspoon ground cinnamon

1 teaspoon cornstarch

About 1 tablespoon cold water

1 teaspoon lemon zest, chopped

1 tablespoon Kirsch (optional)

Place the cherries and the apple juice in a medium nonreactive saucepan. Cook over medium heat until the liquid begins to boil. Boil gently for about 5 minutes or until the cherries plump up, indicating they have been cooked thoroughly. Taste the liquid for sweetness and add the maple syrup to adjust. Add the cinnamon and cook for another minute.

Meanwhile, in a small bowl, dissolve the cornstarch in about 1 tablespoon cold water, stirring until smooth. While stirring the cherry mixture constantly, pour in the cornstarch and let the mixture return to a boil. Immediately remove from the heat and stir in the lemon zest and the Kirsch, if desired. Serve hot, room temperature, or cold. The sauce will keep for about 5 days if refrigerated in an airtight container.

Strawberry Rhubarb Sauce

Makes about 4 cups

Whether this is used for a tart filling or a cheesecake topping, this is a classic combination of flavors. You can adjust the amount of sweetener to suit your own taste. I prefer my sauces to be more tart than sweet.

When cooking with both strawberries and rhubarb, remember that they will cook down considerably, if you let them. I like to let the rhubarb dissolve. I add the berries last, cooking them only briefly so they keep their shape.

3 cups strawberries, hulled and sliced in half

⅓ cup Sucanat, honey, or maple syrup

2 cups cubed rhubarb

¼ cup water

2 tablespoons cornstarch

2 tablespoons cold water

¼ cup fresh orange juice

2 teaspoons orange zest, finely chopped

In a medium nonreactive bowl, sprinkle the sliced strawberries with 2 tablespoons of sweetener. Let the berries sit while cooking the rhubarb.

In a medium saucepan, cook the rhubarb and water over medium heat stirring as necessary. As the rhubarb cooks, it will produce a lot of liquid. Once it begins to cook down, stir in some of the remaining sweetener.

Continue cooking until the rhubarb has dissolved into a sauce. Add the sweetened strawberries with all of their juice. Taste the mixture and adjust for sweetness. Continue cooking for another minute.

To thicken the mixture, in a small bowl, dissolve the cornstarch in 2 tablespoons cold water until smooth. Stir into the sauce and bring to a boil. Remove from the heat. Add the orange juice and the zest. Serve warm or chilled.

Foundations and Finishing Touches

Sweet Cherry Sauce

Makes about 2 cups

Once you taste sauce or pies made from summer-fresh cherries and not those from a can or jar, you will know the time spent pitting them is worth every second. This sauce is slightly thickened, and finished with a little butter and Kirsch. Try spooning it over vanilla ice cream or serving it with the Rum and Raisin Ricotta Cake (page 86).

2½ cups pitted Bing cherries
1 cup apple juice, not from concentrate
3 to 4 tablespoons maple syrup
⅛ teaspoon cinnamon
1 tablespoon cornstarch
2 tablespoons cold water
1 teaspoon unsalted butter (optional)
1 tablespoon Kirsch (optional)

Place the cherries and the apple juice in a medium nonreactive saucepan. Cook over medium heat until liquid begins to boil. Boil gently until the cherries plump up, indicating they have been cooked thoroughly, about 5 minutes. Taste the liquid for sweetness and add the maple syrup to adjust. Add the cinnamon and cook for another minute.

Meanwhile, in a small bowl, dissolve the cornstarch in about 2 tablespoons cold water, stirring until smooth. While stirring the cherry mixture constantly, pour in the cornstarch and let the mixture return to a boil. Immediately remove from the heat and stir in the butter and the Kirsch, if desired. Serve hot, room temperature, or cold. The sauce will keep refrigerated in an airtight container for about 5 days.

Sweet Tart Pastry

Makes one 10-inch-round single-crust tart shell

This is the perfect crust when you need a cookie-like base for custard fillings.
If you prefer, you can increase the flour by ⅓ cup and eliminate the nuts.

1⅓ cups unbleached all-purpose flour
¼ cup ground almonds
½ teaspoon baking powder
⅓ cup maple sugar
Pinch of salt
1 large egg, lightly beaten
½ cup (1 stick) unsalted butter, at room temperature

Have ready one 10-inch tart pan with a removable bottom.

In a large bowl, combine the flour, almonds, baking powder, maple sugar, and salt. Add the beaten egg and blend, using your hands until the mixture resembles coarse meal. Add the butter and blend until you have a smooth dough. Wrap in plastic wrap and chill for at least 1 hour.

Position one rack in the lower part of your oven and another in the middle part of the oven. Preheat the oven to 350°F.

On a lightly floured work surface, roll the pastry to ⅛-inch thick. Line the tart pan with the dough. Trim any excess dough from the sides. Use the tines of a fork to pierce the bottom of the tart shell in several places. Freeze for 10 minutes. Bake for 15 to 20 minutes, or until the pastry is lightly browned.

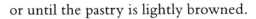

SOURCE LIST

Maple sugar and syrup

Butternut Mountain Farm
Johnson, Vermont 05656
Tel: (800) 828-2376

Timian's Maple Farms
Timian Road
Sauquoit, New York 13456
Tel: (800) 779-0316

Quebec Maple Syrup Producers'
Federation
boul. Roland-Therrien
Longueuil, Quebec J4H 3Y9
Tel: (514) 679-0530
Fax: (514) 679-0139

Date sugar

Seaview Ranch Date Products
Johnson St.
Thermal, California 92274
Tel: (619) 397-2200
Fax: (619) 397-4187

Brown rice syrup

Lundberg Family Farms
Church St., Box 369
Richvale, California 95974-0369
Tel: (916) 882-4551
Fax: (916) 882-4500

Sucanat

Sucanat
P.O. Box 2860, Fentness Blvd.
Daytona Beach, Florida 32120
Tel: (904) 947-4707
Fax: (904) 258-4707

FruitSource

FruitSource
Mission St., Suite 404
Santa Cruz, CA 95060
Tel: (408) 457-1136

Barley malt syrup

Eden Foods, Inc.
Clinton, Michigan 49236
Tel: (517) 456-7424

Naturally sweetened chocolate products

Sunspire Grain-Sweetened
Chocolate Chips
Tel: (510) 569-9731
Fax: (510) 568-4948

Tropical Source
c/o Cloud Nine, Inc.
Hoboken, New Jersey 07030
Tel: (201) 216-0382
Fax: (201) 216-0383

Naturally sweetened graham crackers and other products

Hain Pure Foods Co., Inc.
Uniondale, New York 11553
Tel: (516) 257-6200

INDEX

a

Almond Torte, 61–62
Apple(s), about, 153
  baked, 46
  Crisp, 42–43
  Custard Tart, 151
  Fritters, 183–84
  Orange Caramel Cake, 62–63
  Pie, 152–53
  poached, 55–56
  Rhubarb Crisp, 44
  -Rosemary Pizza, 186–87
Applesauce, 45
Apricot(s)
  Crumb Cake, 64–65
  honey poached, 49
  Mascarpone Ice Cream, 123
  Pastry Cream, 211
  roasted, 58
  Sorbet, 124
Arborio Rice Pudding, 125
Aunt Josephine's Chocolate Cake, 66–67

B

Bain-marie, about, 24
Baked Apples, 46
Baklava, walnut, 179–80
Banana
  Bread Pudding, 10–11
  Chocolate Crêpes, 188–89
  Cream Tart with Dark Chocolate
    Sauce, 154–55
  Kahlúa Ice Cream, 126
  pecan caramel fritters, 202–3
  Raisin Bran Muffins, 12
  strawberry yogurt smoothy, 137
  Walnut Bread, 13

Barley malt syrup, about, 5
Basmati Rice Pudding, 127
Berry Hazelnut Crumb Cake, 69–70
Biscuits, lemon–sweet potato, 27–28
Blackberry, hazelnut linzertorte, 77–78
Black Forest Crêpes, 185
Black Plum Kuchen, 70–71
Black Raspberry Ripple Ice Cream,
  128–29
Blind baking, about, 157
Blintzes, blueberry cheese, 14–15
Blood Orange Currant Cookies, 95–96
Blood Orange Sorbet, 129
Blueberry
  Cheese Blintzes, 14–15
  Cornmeal Pancakes, 16
  Corn Muffins, 15
  Gooseberry Crumb Pie, 156–57
  lemon muffins, 25
  -Nectarine Cornbread Cobbler,
    47–48
  Pie, 158
  Sauce, 212
Bourbon ice cream, 133
Breads, 13, 40, 108–9
Brownie cookies, 99
Brownies, Sonny's chocolate
  walnut, 120
Brown rice syrup, about, 5
Buns, cinnamon pecan, 19–21
Butter, clarified, 189
Butter Cookies, 97
Buttercream, French, 220–21
Buttercream, Italian meringue chocolate,
  76–77, 224–25
Buttermilk French Toast with Maple
  Syrup Peaches, 17–18
Butternut Squash Custard, 130
Butternut Squash Tarts, 160
Butter Tarts, 159

C

Cake(s), 38, 60–92. *See also* Cheesecake; Genoise; Gingerbread; Linzertorte; Shortcake; Tiramisu; Tortes
  apple orange caramel, 62–63
  chocolate, Aunt Josephine's, 66–67
  cornmeal, 74–75
  crumb, 64–65, 69–70
  devil's food, 76–77
  marble pound, 38–39
  orange layer, 81
  orange poppy seed, 84–85
  prune and rum, 88–89
  rum and raisin ricotta, 86–87
Caramel
  apple, orange cake, 62–63
  Custard, 131–32
  Grand Marnier–, gelato, 143
  -pear sauce, 90–92
  pecan, banana fritters, 202–3
Caramelizing maple syrup, 132
Cardamom, poached apples with orange and, 55–56
Cashew Butter Thumbprint Cookies, 98
Cheesecake, lemon, 82–83
Cherry
  Kumquat Compote, 48–49
  sauces, 230, 232
  tarts, 166–67
Chocolate
  Bourbon Ice Cream, 133
  Brownie Espresso Chip Cookies, 99
  buttercream, Italian meringue, 76–77, 224–25
  cakes, 66–67, 76–77
  chip cookies, 101, 107
  Coconut Cream Pie, 162–63
  crêpes, 188–89, 213
  Pastry, 214
  Pecan Pie, 164
  –Pine Nut Tart, 165
  sauces, dark, 154–55, 218
  Shortbread, 102–3

  walnut brownies, 120
  -Walnut Cigars, 175
Cinnamon, pear, ice cream, 146–47
Cinnamon Pecan Sticky Buns, 19–21
Clarified butter, about, 189
Cobblers, 47–48, 52–53
Coconut, chocolate cream pie, 162–63
Coconut-Strawberry Shortcake, 72–73
Compotes, 48–49, 54
Cookies, 94–120
  blood orange currant, 95–96
  butter, 97
  cashew butter, 98
  chocolate brownie espresso chip, 99
  chocolate chip, 101, 107
  chocolate shortbread, 102–3
  cream cheese, 103–4
  oatmeal raisin, 112
  orange gingersnaps, 113
  peanut butter, 114, 116–17
Cornbread cobbler, blueberry-nectarine, 47–48
Cornmeal, blueberry, pancakes, 16
Cornmeal Cake with Honey-Rosemary Syrup and Raspberries, 74–75
Coulis, black raspberry, 198–99
Cranberry, orange muffins, 30–31
Cream
  apricot pastry, 211
  espresso butter, 79–80
  lemon whipped, 90–92
  orange mascarpone, 50
  pastry, 228
Cream cheese
  cookies, 103–4
  icing, honey lemon, 217
Creaming technique, 100
Cream puffs, 190, 229
Crème Anglaise, 215
Crème fraîche, about, 163
Crêpes, 185, 188–89, 213, 216–17
Crusts, 219, 233
Curd, lime, 223
Currant, blood orange, cookies, 95–96

Currant, orange, scones, 32–33
Custard(s), 130, 131–32, 151
  sauce, 215

D

Dark Chocolate Sauce, 218
Date Nut Steamed Pudding, 191
Date Squares, 105–6
Date sugar, about, 6
Devil's Food Cake with Italian Meringue
  Chocolate Buttercream, 76–77
Double Chocolate Chip Cookies, 107
Double Sour Cherry Tarts, 166–67
Dough, about, 33, 171
Doughnuts, jelly, 22–24

E

Espresso butter cream, hazelnut torte
  with, 79–80
Espresso chip cookies, chocolate
  brownie, 99

F

Fig and Frangipane Tarts, 168
Figs sautéed with pine nuts, 201
Figs with orange mascarpone, 50
Frangipanes, 168, 221
French Buttercream, 220–21
French toast, buttermilk, 17–18
Fritters, 183–84, 202–3
Fruit salad, orange blossom-scented, 51
Fruit Soup, 192
FruitSource, about, 7

G

Galette, rhubarb, 176–77. See also Fig
  and Frangipone Tarts
Gelatos, 140, 143
Genoise, 222–23
Ginger
  pear-, strudel, 172–73
  pineapple-, sorbet, 145

and plum strudel, 178–79
  poached pears with wine and, 57–58
Gingerbread, upside-down pear, 90–92
Gingersnaps, orange, 113
Gluten, about, 26
Gooseberry, blueberry, crumb pie, 156–57
Graham Cracker Crust, 219
Grand Marnier–Caramel Gelato, 143
Granola, 18

H

Hazelnut(s)
  berry, crumb cake, 69–70
  Blackberry Linzertorte, 77–78
  Frangipane, 221
  toasting, 83
  Torte with Espresso Butter Cream,
    79–80
Honey, about, 4–5
  Lemon Cream Cheese Icing, 88–89, 217
  Mousse with Spiced Plum Sauce,
    134–35
  Poached Apricots, 49
  -rosemary syrup, 74–75

I

Ice cream
  apricot mascarpone, 123
  banana Kahlúa, 126
  black raspberry ripple, 128–29
  chocolate bourbon, 133
  lemon strawberry, 136
  lychee, 138
  malt, 139
  Ouzo, 144–45
  pear cinnamon, 146–47
Icing, honey lemon cream cheese,
  88–89, 217
Imbibing syrup, 194
Italian Meringue Chocolate Buttercream,
  76–77, 224–25

J

Jelly Doughnuts, 22–24

K

Kahlúa, banana ice cream, 126
Kuchen, black plum, 70–71
Kumquat, cherry compote, 48–49

L

Lemon
    Blueberry Muffins, 25
    Cheesecake with Strawberry Rhubarb
        Sauce, 82–83
    honey, cream cheese icing, 88–89, 217
    Meringue Pie, 169
    Rice Cakes, 193
    Strawberry Ice Cream, 136
    -Sweet Potato Biscuits, 27–28
    Tart, 170
    whipped cream, 90–92
Lime Curd, 223
Lime Trifle, 194
Linzertorte, hazelnut blackberry, 77–78
Lokshen Kugel, 195
Lychee Ice Cream, 138

M

Macaroons, 106
Malt Ice Cream, 139
Mandel Bread, 108–9
Mango, bread, spiced, 40
Mango Gelato, 140
Mango Yogurt Mousse, 141
Maple sugar, about, 3–4, 67
Maple syrup, about, 3, 132
    Mousse, 142
    peaches, 17–18
Mascarpone cheese, about, 50
    apricot ice cream, 123
    figs with orange and, 50
Melon Soup, 196–97
Meringue, Italian, chocolate buttercream,
    76–77, 224–25
Meringue, lemon, pie, 169
Mincemeat Turnovers, 110–11
Molasses, about, 6

Molasses Raisin Bran Muffins, 28–29
Mousses, 134–35, 141, 142, 148
Muffins, 12, 15, 25, 28–29, 30–31, 31–32

Nectarine, blueberry-, cornbread cobbler,
    47–48
Noodle pudding, 195

Oatmeal Nutmeg Pancakes, 29–30
Oatmeal Pear Muffins, 31–32
Oatmeal Raisin Cookies, 112
Orange
    apple, caramel cake, 62–63
    blood, currant cookies, 95–96
    blood, sorbet, 129
    Blossom-Scented Fruit Salad, 51
    and cardamom, poached apples with,
        55–56
    Cranberry Muffins, 30–31
    Currant Scones, 32–33
    Gingersnaps, 113
    Layer Cake, 81
    mascarpone cream, fresh figs with, 50
    Polenta Pudding with Black Raspberry
        Coulis, 198–99
    Poppy Seed Cake, 84–85
    -Tarragon Sorbet, 144
Ouzo Ice Cream, 144–45

P

Pancakes, 16, 29–30
Panettone, 34–37
Panettone Bread Pudding, 200
Pastry, 226–27
    chocolate, 214
    creams, 211, 228
    sweet tart, 233
Pâte à Choux, 229
Peaches, maple syrup, French toast with,
    17–18
Peach Raspberry Cobbler, 52–53

Peanut Butter Cookies, 114
Peanut Butter Squares, 116–17
Peanuts and Popcorn, 197
Pear(s)
    Cinnamon Ice Cream, 146–47
    gingerbread, upside-down, 90–92
    -Ginger Strudel, 172–73
    oatmeal, muffins, 31–32
    poached, with fresh ginger and wine,
        57–58
Pecan, cinnamon buns, 19–21
Pecan Caramel Banana Fritters,
    202–3
Pecan pie, chocolate, 164
Phyllo, about, 174
Pies, 152–53, 156–7, 158, 162–63,
    164, 169
Pineapple Compote, 54
Pineapple-Ginger Sorbet, 145
Pine nut, chocolate–, tart, 165
Pine nuts, figs with, 201
Piping tube, making a, 115
Pizza, apple-rosemary, 186–87
Plum, black, kuchen, 70–71
Plum and ginger strudel, 178–79
Plum sauce, spiced, 134–35
Poached Apples with Orange and
    Cardamom, 55–56
Poached Pears with Fresh Ginger and
    Wine, 57–58
Polenta pudding, 198–99
Popcorn, peanuts and, 197
Poppy seed cake, 84–85
Prune and rum cake, 88–89
Puddings, 10, 11, 125, 127, 191, 195,
    198–99, 200, 204–5
    bread, 10–11, 200
    rice, 125, 127
Pumpkin Steamed Pudding, 204–5

R

Raisin
    bran muffins, 12, 28–29
    oatmeal, cookies, 112
    rum and, ricotta cake, 86–87

Raspberry(ies)
    black, coulis, 198–99
    black, ripple ice cream, 128–29
    cornmeal cake with, 74–75
    Mousse, 148
    peach cobbler, 52–53
Rhubarb
    apple crisp, 44
    Galette, 176–77
    strawberry sauce, 82–83, 231
Rice cakes, lemon, 193
Roasted Apricots, 58
Roasted Plum and Ginger Strudel, 178–79
Rugelach, 118–19
Rum and prune cake, 88–89
Rum and Raisin Ricotta Cake, 86–87

S

Salad, fruit, 51
Sauce(s)
    apple, 45
    blueberry, 212
    caramel-pear, 90–92
    cherry, 230, 232
    chocolate, dark, 154–55, 218
    ripple, 128
    plum, spiced, 134–35
    strawberry rhubarb, 82–83, 231
Sautéed Figs with Pine Nuts, 201
Scones, orange currant, 32–33
Shortbread, chocolate, 102–3
Shortcake, coconut-strawberry, 72–73
Sonny's Chocolate Walnut Brownies, 120
Sorbets, 124, 129, 137, 144, 145
Soups, 192, 196–97
Sour Cherry Sauce, 230
Sour Cream Marble Pound Cake, 38–39
Spiced Mango Bread, 40
Spiced Prune and Rum Cake with Honey
    Lemon Cream Cheese Icing, 88–89
Squash, about, 161
    butternut, 130, 160
Strawberry
    Banana Yogurt Smoothy, 137
    -coconut shortcake, 72–73

Strawberry (*cont.*)
   lemon ice cream, 136
   Rhubarb Sauce, 82–83, 231
   Sorbet, 137
Strudels, 172–73, 178–79
Sucanat, about, 6–7
Sweet Cherry Sauce, 232
Sweet potato, lemon-, biscuits, 27–28
Sweet Tart Pastry, 233

T

Tart(s)
   apple custard, 151
   banana cream, 154–55
   butter, 159
   butternut squash, 160
   chocolate–pine nut, 165
   fig and frangipane, 168
   lemon, 170
   sour cherry, 166–67
Tiramisu, 206–7
Tortes, 61–62, 79–80

Trifle, lime, 194
Turnovers, mincemeat, 110–11

U

Upside-Down Pear Gingerbread with
   Caramel-Pear Sauce and Lemon
   Whipped Cream, 90–92

W

Walnut
   Baklava, 179–80
   banana bread, 13
   chocolate-, cigars, 175
   chocolate brownies, 120
Whipping cream, about, 68
Whole wheat flour, about, 26
Wine, poached pears with, 57–58

Y

Yogurt desserts, 137, 141

CPSIA information can be obtained at www.ICGtesting.com
Printed in the USA
BVOW061308301212

309177BV00007B/411/P